E. Berkley

The Pharaohs and Their People

Scenes of Old Egyptian Life and History

E. Berkley

The Pharaohs and Their People
Scenes of Old Egyptian Life and History

ISBN/EAN: 9783337227319

Printed in Europe, USA, Canada, Australia, Japan

Cover: Foto ©ninafisch / pixelio.de

More available books at **www.hansebooks.com**

SCENES OF OLD EGYPTIAN LIFE AND HISTORY

BY

E. BERKLEY

AUTHOR OF 'A HISTORY OF ROME,' ETC. ETC.

With Numerous Illustrations

SEELEY, JACKSON & HALLIDAY, FLEET STREET

LONDON, MDCCCLXXXIV

The growing interest that is felt in all that concerns Egypt and its past has led me to hope that there may be many who will be glad of a book containing, in a concise and easily accessible form, the chief results of modern research and discovery in the valley of the Nile.

The Manuscript of this work was submitted to Dr. Lushington, formerly Professor of Greek at Glasgow University, and he has very kindly permitted the publication of the following opinion :—

'It appears to me very carefully and accurately written, with diligent consultation of the most trustworthy sources. The illustrative quotations interspersed seem well calculated to inspire and maintain interest in the reader as well as the descriptive sketches.

'The subject well deserves, and is already beginning to command, more general interest than a few years ago it would have been possible to anticipate.'

The translations I have given are selected and freely rendered from those that have appeared in *Records of the Past*, after comparison with any others that were available. I am also much indebted throughout to Dr. Brugsch's valuable *History of Egypt;* and I wish especially to mention my obligation to Mr. Villiers Stuart's *Nile Gleanings*, with its many interesting illustrations and accompanying descriptions—more particularly those relating to the tombs of the third and fourth dynasties, to the curious episode of Khu-en-aten's reign, and to the stirring times of Rameses the Great.

My obligations to other authors are acknowledged in the respective places.

The hieroglyphs above the Table of Contents read, *em rek suteniu tepau*, *i.e.* 'in the time of former kings,' and the cartouche at the end of the line is that of 'Pharaoh,' to be read *Per-aa*, *i.e.* 'the Great House.' The hawk is symbolic of divine protection, and the seal it holds is the emblem of renewed and endless life.

E. BERKLEY.

CONTENTS.

CHAPTER I.
Reign of the gods—Osiris, Isis, and Horus Myth—Ancient Cities and early Kings, ... 1

CHAPTER II.
The Pyramid Builders, ... 17

CHAPTER III.
The Pyramid Builders—*continued*, ... 29

CHAPTER IV.
Civil War and Break-up of the Kingdom—Reunion and Recovery, 41

CHAPTER V.
Twelfth Dynasty—'Instructions' of Amenemhat I.—Story of Saneha, ... 49

CHAPTER VI.
Successors of Amenemhat I.—Two Provinces added to Egypt, . 64

CHAPTER VII.
Invasion and Rule of the Hyksos—War of Liberation. (*Circa* 2100-1600 B.C.), ... 79

CHAPTER VIII.

The Eighteenth Dynasty—Queen Hatasu and Thothmes III. (*Circa* 1600-1400 B.C.), ... 88

CHAPTER IX.

The Eighteenth Dynasty—*continued*. (*Circa* 1600-1400 B.C.), . 125

CHAPTER X.

The Nineteenth Dynasty (*circa* 1400-1200 B.C.)—Rameses the Great, ... 142

CHAPTER XI.

Thebes; its People, Temples, and Tombs—Close of the Nineteenth Dynasty, ... 175

CHAPTER XII.

Twentieth and Twenty-first Dynasties—**The Ramessidæ and the Priest-Kings.** (*Circa* 1200-970 B.C.), . . . 212

CHAPTER XIII.

Shishak I. and the Twenty-second (Bubastite) Dynasty—The Ethiopian Kings—The Assyrians in Egypt—Sack of Thebes. (*Circa* 970-666 B.C.), ... 237

CHAPTER XIV.

Psammetichus and the Saite Dynasty—The Persian Conquest— Last Independent Dynasties. (666-340 B.C.), . . 263

APPENDIX I.—Table of **Dynasties,** 288
APPENDIX II.—Decipherment of the Hieroglyphs, . . 290

LIST OF ILLUSTRATIONS.

TAI-TI, QUEEN OF AMENHOTEP III.,	*Frontispiece*
WINGED FIGURE,—ISIS OR NEPHTHYS,	PAGE 2
ISIS SUCKLING HORUS,	4
THE SPHINX,	18
THE PYRAMIDS,	23
NETTING BIRDS,	31
CARESSING A GAZELLE,	63
BOATMEN AND CATTLE-DRIVERS,	68
PAINTING A STATUE,	72
CARVING A STATUE,	73
ASIATIC IMMIGRANTS,	76
AMENHOTEP PRESENTED TO AMEN-RA BY HORUS,	118
AMENHOTEP II. ON THE LAP OF A GODDESS,	122
AMENHOTEP III.,	128
THE COLOSSI AT THEBES,	129
RAMESES II.,	162
HALL IN THE GREAT TEMPLE OF ABU-SIMBEL,	166
DISCOVERY OF MUMMIES AT DEIR EL BAHARI,	173
TEMPLE AND GARDEN,	177
THE SACRED ARK,	181
PLAYING AT DRAUGHTS,	184
THE WEIGHING OF ACTIONS,	193
MUMMY AND MUMMY-CASE OF THE PRIEST NEBSENI,	231
MUMMY OF A GAZELLE,	235
THE WORSHIP OF APIS,	244
SPHINX WITH HUMAN HANDS,	287

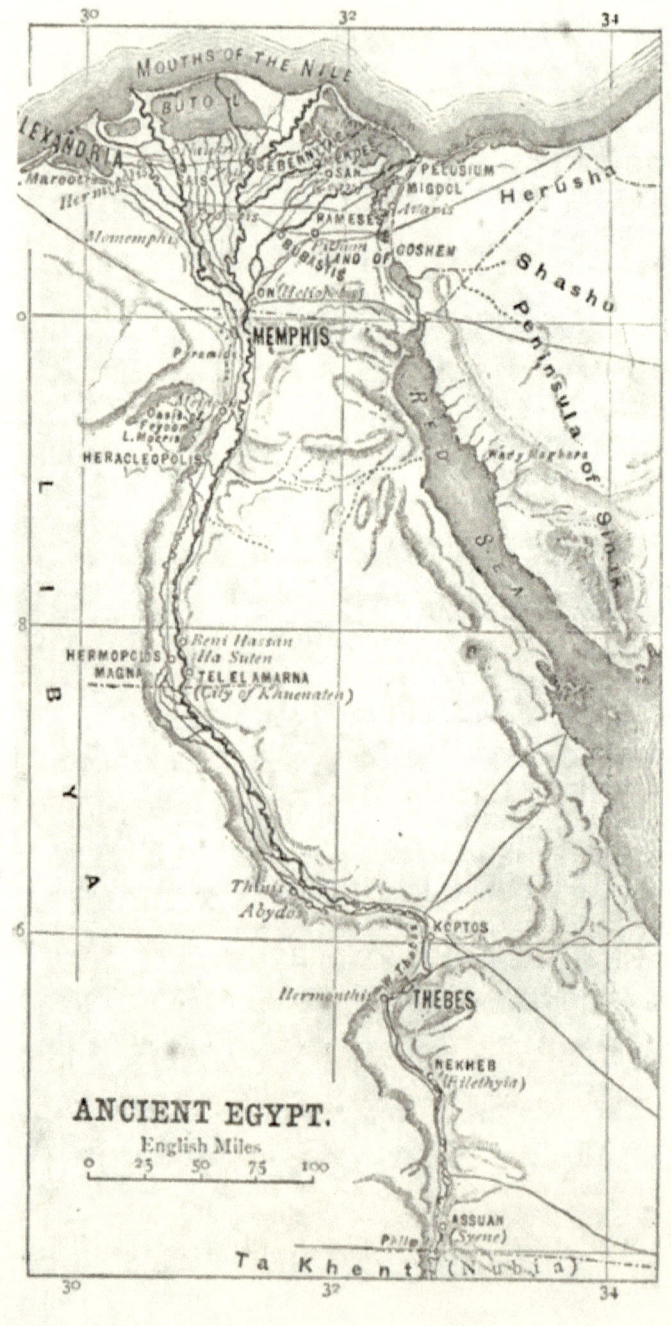

THE PHARAOHS AND THEIR PEOPLE.

CHAPTER I.

Reign of the gods—Osiris, Isis, and Horus Myth—Ancient cities and early kings.

THE first royal name that meets us on the monuments of Egypt, which was inscribed there during the lifetime of the king who bore it, is that of Senefru (predecessor of Khufu who built the Great Pyramid), and belongs to a remote antiquity.[1] And yet we must look back through the dimness of many more centuries still before we come to the name of Mena, first King of Egypt—a name that seems to twinkle faintly from beyond the abyss of long

---

[1] The date that has been assigned to the Great Pyramid varies by at least a thousand years, and is generally placed from about 3000 to 4000 B.C. The present tendency is certainly rather in favour of the remoter dates, as agreeing best with the requirements of historic data, and harmonising with the results of recent discovery and research.

past ages like a far-off star on the horizon from beyond the wide waste of waters.

Mena, founder of Memphis, and his successors, we know, at least, by name; but of the 'old time before them' the traditions of Egypt only said that the gods governed the land. According to one ancient record, Ptah, the 'Hidden Being,' the 'Former of all,' ruled in the beginning; Ra, the bright Sun-god, Seb, the ancient Earth-god, followed; and later still Osiris reigned, the 'Good Being' and 'Lord of life.' After having conferred manifold blessings and benefits on the land, he was slain by his brother and rival Set. Set concealed the body, but Isis, the 'great divine Mother,' sister and wife of Osiris, sought after it. An ancient hymn says, 'No word of hers fails; good is she, and kind in will and speech. It is Isis, the exalted one, the avenger of her brother: she went up and down the world lamenting him.'

The *Lamentations of Isis* was one of the most revered of the sacred writings:—'My heart is full of bitterness for thee,' she cries; 'how long will it be ere I see thee whom to behold is bliss! Come to her that loveth thee

WINGED FIGURE, ISIS OR NEPHTHYS.

—none hath loved thee more than I. . . . Heaven and earth are mourning after thee. O mighty one, our lord,[1] speak, and dispel the anguish of our souls! To behold thy face is life, and the joy of our spirits is to gaze on thee!'

Nevertheless in bodily form Osiris appeared not on earth again; but Isis ceased not from her search until she had found the remains, all torn and mangled as they were by the malice of Set. 'She made light with her feathers,' says the old hymn, 'and wind with her wings; at his burial she poured forth her prayers.'

'She gave birth to a child; secretly and alone she nursed the infant—no man knows where that was done.

'Now has the arm of that child become strong within the ancient dwelling of Seb.'[2]

The child of Isis, the beautiful and radiant Horus, was the avenger of Osiris; he cast down the terrible Set, and destroyed his power; then, on appearing resplendent from his triumph, he was hailed with acclamation by gods and

---

[1] Isis is joined in her lamentations by her sister Nephthys, who was wife of Set, but never shared his evil repute.

[2] *i.e.* The Earth. Seb, the Earth-god, was father of Osiris; Nut, the Heaven above, was his mother in Egyptian mythology.

men, and reigned over the land, Osiris, new-born—the Morning Sun which, having conquered night and darkness, ascends the sky and rules from heaven; the Sun of to-day,

Isis suckling Horus.—From a statuette in the British Museum.

which, if another, is yet the same as that which sank down yesterday into the bosom of the night.

The reign of Horus was welcomed with rapture and with song. 'He receives the title of his father and rules the world; he governs both the men of Egypt and the northern barbarians. Every one glorifies his goodness; mild is his love towards us; his tenderness embraceth every heart; great is his love in all our bosoms. His foe falls under his fury; the end of the evil-doer is at hand. The son of Isis, the avenger of his father, appears. The worlds are at rest; evil flies, and earth brings forth abundantly, and is at peace beneath her lord.'

But Osiris was not dead. In the unseen world he lived anew, and there he ruled in righteousness, as Horus ruled on earth. Osiris, the divine being who had died, was judge of the dead. Before him each departed spirit must appear in the judgment hall of Truth. There the heart is weighed and the life is judged unerringly. He who passes that ordeal becomes himself Osiris, and is henceforth called by his name. The new Osiris lives again, and passes victoriously through every peril, until he is at length admitted amongst the bright and blessed spirits who accompany Ra for ever, and who 'live, as he liveth, in Truth.'

Horus was the last of the divine race of kings. After him, some traditions said that dynasties of demigods and of manes ruled before King Mena ascended the throne, but the name by which the Egyptians always distinguished the inhabitants of the land in prehistoric times was *Horshesu*—followers of Horus.

There were certain cities also in Egypt whose foundation was assigned to those prehistoric times. The twin cities Thinis-Abydos were, so far as we know, the most ancient in the land. Thinis was the cradle of the Egyptian monarchy: the first Egyptian dynasties were Thinite, and Mena went from thence to found his new capital. But Abydos was revered as the burial-place and shrine of Osiris himself, and many devout Egyptians in following ages directed their own tombs to be prepared and their bodies laid in this consecrated spot.

The origin of Pa-Ra,[1] the City of the Sun, is also lost in remote antiquity. It stood not

---

[1] In Greek *Heliopolis*, which bears the same meaning as Pa-Ra—'City of the Sun.'

far from Memphis, and is better known to us by the name of On. It was the centre of the worship of Ra, as Abydos was of the worship of Osiris, but there was no jealousy or rivalry between the two. They were, in fact, essentially one, and the same individual might be priest or priestess of both sanctuaries.

On was famous from time immemorial as a seat of learning, and its priesthood was held in high repute. The city itself was of small dimensions. 'The walls may yet be traced,' says Mr. Reginald Stuart Poole, 'enclosing an irregular square of about half a mile in the measure of each of its sides.' And of this limited space the great temple of Ra must have occupied about half. The population, one would think, must have been mainly composed of scholars, as the priests' dwellings would be within the temple precincts. Hither came the young men of Egypt—who shall say how many thousand years ago!—to learn all that the priests could teach at this, the most ancient university of the world. Nor were the priests, who carefully cultivated and taught the various branches of learning, by any means an exclusive caste.

They had family ties, mixed in social life, and could hold other than priestly dignities. A royal prince was often priest of a temple, and a priest might be a warrior, an architect, or a court official. So far as we can gather, the teaching at an Egyptian university would comprise a knowledge of the sacred books, besides general teaching in morality. The study of the language itself must have been a somewhat arduous undertaking even for a native-born Egyptian, and to write the hieroglyphic characters, required considerable skill, and even art.[1] Many branches of science must have been pursued—medicine, law, geometry, astronomy, and chemistry, whilst in mechanics a quite marvellous proficiency was attained. Music too was highly prized and carefully taught, and it is not unlikely that architects and sculptors also received their training in these schools.

Long ages afterwards, when Greek and Roman travellers visited Egypt, and sought to

---

[1] So much was this the case, that at a later period simpler forms of writing, known as the hieratic and demotic were adopted for general purposes; but the ancient hieroglyphic characters continued to be employed on monuments and in the temples.

learn her wisdom, they heard an ancient tale concerning the mysterious Phœnix, that came once in five hundred years from the far-off land of spices and perfume to the sacred City of the Sun, where he constructed for himself a funeral pile and perished in the flames, but only to rise again in renewed life and splendour; then, spreading his radiant wings, he took his flight to the distant land from whence he came. What special truth this allegory veiled in the minds of those who told it we can only guess; at the same time it may serve us well as a type of the old 'wisdom' itself,[1] which did not perish with its primeval seat, but sprang into renewed and glorious existence in what, to us, is 'ancient' Greece—then, lost again when Greece was lost, revived once more in our latter days.

But Pa-Ra had a special claim to the veneration of the Egyptians as the birthplace of their sacred literature. Here were written, or, as the priests called it, 'found,' the original

---

[1] This comparison of the ancient 'wisdom' to the phœnix is taken from Reginald Stuart Poole's *Cities of Egypt*,—an interesting and suggestive book, to which I have been more than once indebted, and especially in the above description of On.

chapters of the most sacred of the sacred writings, the '*Book of the coming forth into the Day*,'[1] which tells of the conflicts and triumphs of the life after death.

To secure that triumph, a knowledge of the holy book was required. Portions of it are found written on coffin lids and on the walls of tombs; every Egyptian desired to have it buried with him, and whilst the rich would often have an entire copy laid in his tomb, the poor man coveted at least a fragment.

Memphis was founded by the first King of Egypt, but Abydos and On were linked by tradition to the gods.

One beautiful obelisk of red granite stands solitary among the green fields to mark where stood the City of the Sun, and the wild bees store their honey in its deep-cut hieroglyphs.

If any remains at all exist of Abydos, they have long since been buried deep beneath the piled up heaps of sand and mud amongst which has been built a little Arab village named 'Arabat the Buried.' Whilst exploring

---

[1] Generally known as the 'Book' or 'Ritual of the Dead,' but it was never known to the Egyptians by any name of the kind.

these mounds the famous discoverer Mariette found two temples erected by well-known kings of far later date, Seti I. and Rameses the Great, and dedicated by them to Osiris. Not far off there arises amid the desolation a conical hillock sixty feet high, which is called by the Arabs Kom-es-Sultan, the 'Mound of the King.' It is just made up of tombs 'packed together as closely as they can be wedged,' above a rock which was believed to have been the sepulchre of Osiris. Here it was that so many during many generations desired to be laid; through the excavations of explorers may be seen countless numbers of the tombs where they hoped to rest in peace. But the mummy cases have been rudely dragged to light, despoiled, and rifled of aught they might have contained of commercial value, while the poor mummies themselves are left, often broken into fragments, exposed to the careless gaze of every passer by and to the 'full glare of the noon-day sun.' Pits sunk in the neighbourhood disclose nothing but tombs, 'arches upon arches of brick, each an Egyptian grave.'[1]

[1] Loftie's *Ride in Egypt*.

Mena founded his new capital 360 miles north of Thinis. The Nahsi or Negroes, in the south, were troublesome rather than dangerous neighbours, and the whole length of the Nile valley was protected by the natural defences of the Libyan hills on the west and the Arabian on the east, but the Delta had no such shelter, and through its plains the way to the rich luxuriant valley lay open to an invading force, whether of the fair-haired Libyans from the west or the warlike tribes of the Amu and the Herusha from the east. Memphis was built some miles south of the point where the narrow valley of the Nile opens out into the broad plains of the Delta.[1] Here the river ran near the Libyan hills; so, by Mena's orders, its course was turned aside to gain a wider space for the new city—Mennefer, he called it—the 'secure and beautiful.' He first of all erected a magnificent temple, which he dedicated to Ptah, 'Father of the beginning'

[1] The length of the Nile, from the spot where the Blue and White Nile unite, down to the Mediterranean, is 1800 miles. The valley of the Nile bounded east by the Arabian, west by the Libyan hills, varies in breadth from fourteen to thirty-two miles, but the breadth of the arable land does not exceed nine or ten miles.—Erasmus Wilson's *Egypt of the Past.*

and 'Creator of the world,' of whose worship Memphis continued to be the centre. It was well fortified and guarded against inroads from the north, and protected the entrance to the Nile valley, of which its rulers held the key. And it was fair to look upon, lying along the banks of the great river—with artificial lakes glittering in the cloudless sunshine, and stately temples and palaces embosomed amongst groves of palm, sycamore, and date trees. Thousands of years passed by, and in later days the ruthless tide of war ebbed and flowed around its walls; siege, storm, and havoc did their work—but in spite of all, so late as the 13th century A.D., an Arabian physician who visited the ruins of Memphis tells us that they extended a half-day's journey every way, and he declares that the wonders he beheld were sufficient to confound the mind; no eloquence could describe them. Every new glance, he says, was a new cause of delight. But the work of ruin was not ended in his day—Mahometan fanaticism spares nothing, however time-honoured or beautiful; besides which, the ruins of Memphis proved a convenient quarry for the building of modern Cairo. Thus the 'secure and beautiful' city of King Mena has disappeared at length as utterly as Babylon has done. A few insignificant fragments and blocks are strewn confusedly about, and serve to mark the site. One mighty statue lies prostrate—a colossal figure of Rameses II., erected by himself in front of the temple of Ptah. It is lying on its face in a broad ditch, deserted and alone, save when some wandering Arab passes by, or cattle come to drink of the water which, for most part of the year, fills the trench and submerges the gigantic figure—

> Round the decay
> Of that colossal wreck, boundless and bare,
> The lone and level sands stretch far away.

Of historic details relating to the earliest dynasties next to nothing has been preserved; the kings appear to have been able and enlightened rulers, and encouragers of art and learning. In their days the system of hieroglyphic writing existed, and we are told of works on the healing arts, some of which were composed by the successor of Mena himself, for 'he was a physician.' The earliest chapters of the sacred books were extant, and the art of embalming was already practised, though in a comparatively rude fashion. We are also informed that by a decree of King Bai-en-neter of the second dynasty, women were declared capable of succeeding to the crown—a statement which is only in harmony with all that we know of the position of women in ancient Egypt.[1]

One remarkable monument of these early dynasties remains.

The Libyan hills, running from north to south, form the western boundary of the Nile valley. Along their base there is a rocky platform of considerable breadth, at a height of some 90 or 100 feet above the plain. This vast platform was used as the necropolis of Memphis—*Ank-ta*, 'Land of life,' they called it. For the space of twenty miles in the neighbourhood of the city,

---

[1] That position was in remarkable contrast to the subjection and seclusion of the Asiatic harem, and was superior to that assigned to women in the domestic and social life of Greece itself. The Egyptian was the husband of one wife, and she was regarded as the honoured mistress of the household; the companion, not the slave or inferior, of the man. In sculptures and paintings she is constantly seen sitting by his side; she joins him in receiving and welcoming guests, and freely takes her part in the occupations and enjoyments of social life. In the tombs and memorial chambers of the dead, husband and wife are still represented side by side.

it was covered with groups of pyramids and tombs. In the centre of the most ancient of these stands the pyramid of Sakkara, known as the 'stepped pyramid,' or 'pyramid of degrees,' which is considered as the burial-place of Ata, fourth King of Egypt. In that case, it is the oldest known sepulchre in the world. It is of grand and rugged aspect, about 200 feet in height, and flattened at the summit. The exterior is formed of six rough gigantic steps composed of stones, and nine or ten feet in thickness.

The forms of King Mena and his successors may well appear dreamlike in the dim light by which we discern them; but we seem to perceive that Mena was, at any rate, the first who wore the 'double crown,' which bespoke sovereignty over the whole land; the white upper crown representing dominion over Upper, the red lower one dominion over Lower Egypt. His successors were strong enough to repel invaders, to maintain intact the power they inherited, and thus to transmit to following dynasties the double crown they had received from Mena, the 'Firm' or 'Constant.'

CHAPTER II.

The Pyramid Builders.

THERE is no longer any need to trust to the scanty notices of these early times that occur in writings of later date. Egyptian inscriptions now tell their own story; the monuments begin to speak. In the valley of Wady Maghara, in the peninsula of Sinai, carved upon the rocky precipice, is to be seen King Senefru himself, in the act of striking down an enemy; the accompanying inscription gives the name and titles of the sovereign, and designates him the conqueror of the Mentu, the 'foreigners of the East.'

In these rocky valleys rich mineral treasures had been discovered, valuable copper ore, besides the blue and green precious stones so much prized in Egypt. These mines were explored and worked by labourers sent from Egypt, and the district gradually passed into possession of its kings.

Fortresses were erected and soldiers stationed there to protect the workmen, and temples were erected that all might be carried on under the protection of the gods. This treasure-yielding district was jealously watched and guarded by the Egyptians, who were thus often brought into collision with neighbouring tribes. Nor is Senefru's tablet by any means the sole record of battle and of conquest, for his successors left many such memorials there. It is not, however, by these alone, or by these principally, that their name and fame has been preserved to modern days.

The rocky platform at the foot of the Libyan hills is of unequal breadth; at one spot, near Memphis, it widens considerably, and forms a sort of promontory jutting out into the plain. It was here that the pyramids of Ghizeh rose in their stupendous majesty. Not far off a huge block of limestone rock, bearing probably some accidental resemblance to an animal at rest,[1] was transformed by the skill of the royal architect into the colossal image of a mysterious

---

[1] The face of the Sphinx is 30 feet long and 14 wide. Its body 140, and its front paws 50 feet long. Between the paws was a small sanctuary.

being—a lion with the head of a man wearing the crown and insignia of an Egyptian monarch—symbol of strength, intellect, and royal dignity. He lay in solemn repose, gazing ever towards the east, where arose each morning Horus of the horizon (Hor-em-khu), the bright deity he represented. To the south of the Sphinx (as the Greeks afterwards called the mystic creature), Khufu, successor of Senefru, erected a temple to Isis, 'Queen of the Pyramids,' and to the north a temple to Osiris, 'Lord of the unseen world,'—thus consecrating the whole of that vast city of the dead to the threefold guardianship of Osiris, Isis, and Horus, names so nearly associated in the Egyptian mind with death, the unseen world, and life triumphant and immortal.

Whilst the great image of Horus was being shaped, and the temples of Osiris and Isis were building, Khufu was by no means unmindful of his own sepulchral monument. The colossal pile,—which he named 'Khut' (Splendour of Light),—is known to us by the name of the 'Great Pyramid.'

The building of these royal tombs, the

pyramids, was the work of a lifetime. A square was first formed, the corners of which were exactly north, south, east, and west; course upon course was added as the years went by, but it could be finished off at any given moment. The angles were then filled in with granite or limestone, fitted with absolute exactness, and the whole sloping surface was beautifully polished. As King Khufu reigned for fifty-seven years, it is no wonder that his sepulchral monument should have attained such gigantic proportions. To form any idea of what the pyramids must once have been, we must restore these polished casing-stones which are now all but gone, and have probably been used in the building of Cairo. Now, 'their stripped sides present a rude, disjointed appearance,' but then, the first and second were of 'brilliant white or yellow limestone, the third all glowing with the red granite from the First Cataract,' five hundred miles away. 'Then you must build up or uncover the massive tombs, now broken or choked up with sand, so as to restore the aspect of vast streets of tombs, out of which the Great Pyramid would arise like a cathedral above smaller churches. Lastly, you must enclose two other pyramids with stone precincts and gigantic doorways; and, above all, you must restore the Sphinx as he was in the days of his glory."[1]

Narrow passages lead into the heart of the mighty mass of Khufu's pyramid, which rises on a base of 764 feet to the height of 480 feet. When the traveller has climbed, or crept, to the centre he finds himself in a chamber, the walls of which are composed of polished red granite. Nothing is left there now to tell of the royal builder but his empty sarcophagus, and his name and titles, amongst other scrawls, written by the masons in red ochre on the walls.

Khafra, the successor of Khufu, is made very real to us by the wonderful statue of him which was found uninjured amongst a number of other broken ones of the same monarch, in a deep well near his burial-place. It is of a bright greenish stone, and admirably executed. The king's features are life-like and benign. A hawk, symbol of Ra, not seen in our illustration, stands behind, and embraces his head with its

[1] Stanley's *Sinai and Palestine*.

wings, as if sheltering and protecting the sovereign, who was 'Son of the Sun.'

Khafra's pyramid, called by him Ur, or the Great, is second in size only to that of Khufu. On the upper part of it the original casing-stone still remains.

The third of the pyramids of Ghizeh, that of Menkaura, though only about half the size of the other two, exceeded them both in costliness and splendour; it was cased from top to bottom in brilliant red granite, exquisitely finished.

These ancient pyramids have long ago been rifled for the sake of anything they contained of value, but in the red pyramid a sarcophagus was discovered made of black basalt, beautifully wrought. It was shipped for England, but lost off Gibraltar. Only the wooden case reached London, and was deposited in the British Museum, together with the bones that had been gathered out of poor Menkaura's resting-place, and which doubtless formed part of his skeleton.[1]

Of the monarchs of the succeeding dynasties

[1] On the coffin-lid is a hieroglyphic inscription, which is interesting as showing at how early a period the departed spirit was regarded as one with Osiris. It runs thus: 'O Osiris, King of Egypt, Menkaura,

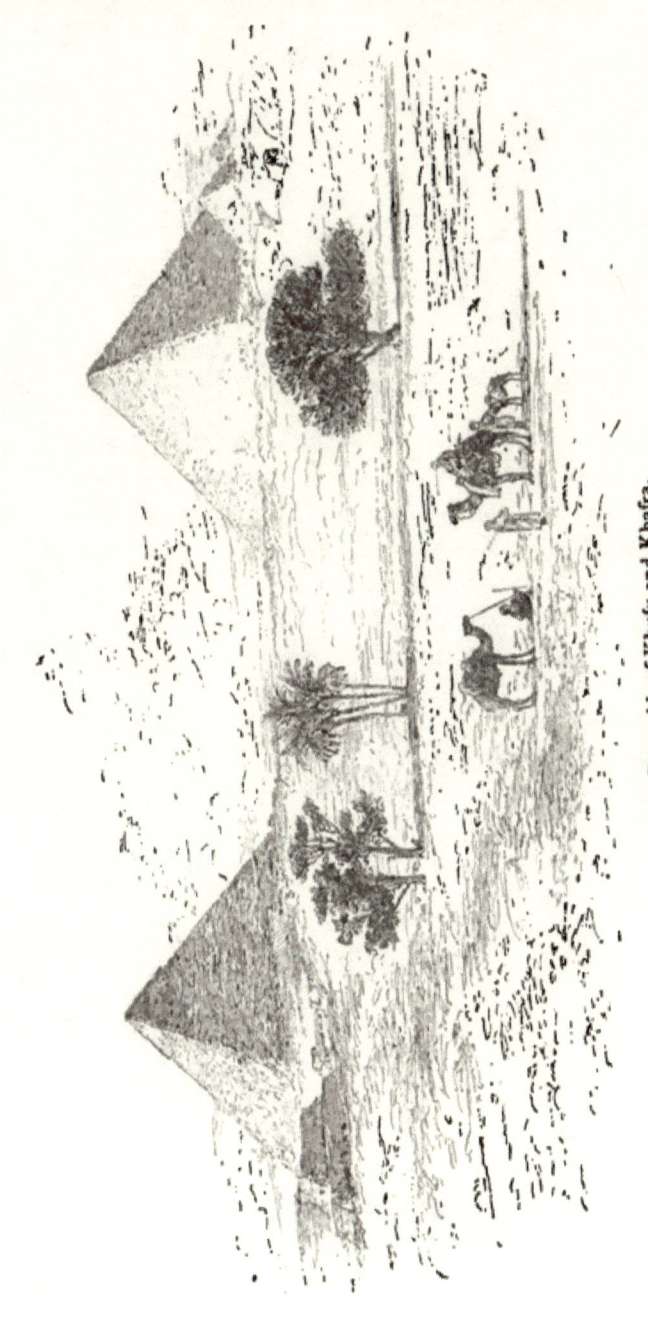

The Pyramids of Khufu and Khafra.

there is little to be said. The names of many of them are found recorded in the valleys of Sinai as 'conquerors of the Mentu,' and they were each and all pyramid builders. The names of their pyramids are known, but only a few of them have been identified.

Recent investigation of the pyramids of Sakkara has brought to light the sepulchres of the last king of the fifth dynasty—Unas—and of Pepi and Merienra of the sixth dynasty, together with their shrivelled remains. From the corpse of the last-named king not only the ornaments, but the coverings and bandages, had been torn away.

Some rays of light are thrown upon the times of Pepi and Merienra by an inscription that was found at Abydos, in the tomb of one Una, who was Governor of the South. In the reign of Teta, first king of the sixth dynasty, Una, then a young man, had been already intrusted with important offices. He was crown-bearer, superintendent of the store-house, and registrar of

living for ever ! born of Heaven, offspring of Seb. May thy Mother Nut (Heaven) stretch herself over thee, and cover thee in her Name of Heavenly Mystery. May she render thee divine, destroying all thine enemies, O King Menkaura, living for ever !

the docks. Under Pepi he rose to yet higher dignity and influence. 'His Majesty gave me the rank of "King's friend;" I was royal scribe and chief over the treasury, and priest of the royal pyramid. No secret was withheld from me; he allowed me to hear all that was said. By his orders I brought a white stone sarcophagus from the land of Ruau. It was embarked safely and brought, together with the doors, cover, and pedestal, in a great boat belonging to the palace.

'But now His Majesty was summoned to drive back the Amu and the Herusha,[1] who were threatening the land. He levied soldiers from beyond the southern frontier, and recruited negroes from very many places. He placed me at the head of these troops. I summoned captains and rulers from every part that they might train and drill the negro forces. I was the representative of the king; everything fell upon me alone, for there was no man above me but Pharaoh himself. To the utmost of my power I laboured; I wore out my sandals in going hither and thither. Never was any army

[1] Tribes inhabiting the desert beyond the north-east frontier of Egypt.

better officered or disciplined. It marched without let or hindrance until it arrived at the land of the Herusha. It laid waste the country, burning the villages, and cutting down vine and fig trees; many thousands of the foe were taken prisoners.

'Five times was I sent to subdue revolts among the Herusha until the land was completely conquered. King Merienra made me Governor of the South, and bestowed high dignity upon me in his household.

'I was charged to bring the sarcophagus and statue for the pyramid of Merienra, and I transported them in boats. I also quarried a great slab of alabaster for the king in seventeen days. I constructed a boat of 100 feet in length, and 50 in breadth. But there was not water enough to tow it in safety. Therefore I excavated four docks in the land of the south, and next year at the time of the inundation I disembarked in safety both the alabaster slab and all the granite required for the pyramid Kha-nefer[1] of Merienra. Then for those docks I erected a building in which the spirits of the king

[1] The Beautiful Rising.

might be invoked, even of the king Merienra, by whose command all had been done that was done.

'The beloved of his father, the praised of his mother, the delight of his brethren, the chief, the Governor of the South, the truly devoted to Osiris—Una.'

CHAPTER III.

The Pyramid Builders—*Continued.*

THE warlike expeditions described by Una, the Governor of the South, form the exception rather than the rule in this early history. Fearing no rivals at home, and almost entirely free from enemies abroad, these powerful monarchs devoted their thoughts and care to the building of temples and of those gigantic funeral piles that have immortalised their names.

It is certain that the pyramids could not have been erected without a very considerable amount of scientific knowledge, whilst as records of engineering skill they are simply marvellous. Immense blocks were brought from a distance of 500 miles up the river, were polished like glass, and fitted into their places with such exactness that the joints could hardly be detected. 'Nothing can be more wonderful,' says

Fergusson, 'than the extraordinary amount of knowledge and perfect precision of execution displayed in the construction of the interior chambers and galleries; nothing more perfect mechanically has ever been executed since.'

A curious calculation has been made that the stone used in the construction of Khufu's pyramid would make a wall of six feet high and half a yard broad, that would reach across the Atlantic from Liverpool to Newfoundland.

In the tombs which cluster round the royal pyramids have been discovered records and relics of deeper and more human interest than the pyramids themselves. At Meidoom were buried the great men of Senefru's time. Their tombs were formed of immense blocks of stone, and have been long hidden from sight by the accumulation of soil above them. The entrance passages are covered with figures and inscriptions. The figures are wrought in a kind of mosaic work. Little square holes were made, and filled with hard cement of various colours. The brightness of the tints is wonderful, as if they had been laid on yesterday; and in some places there can be discerned

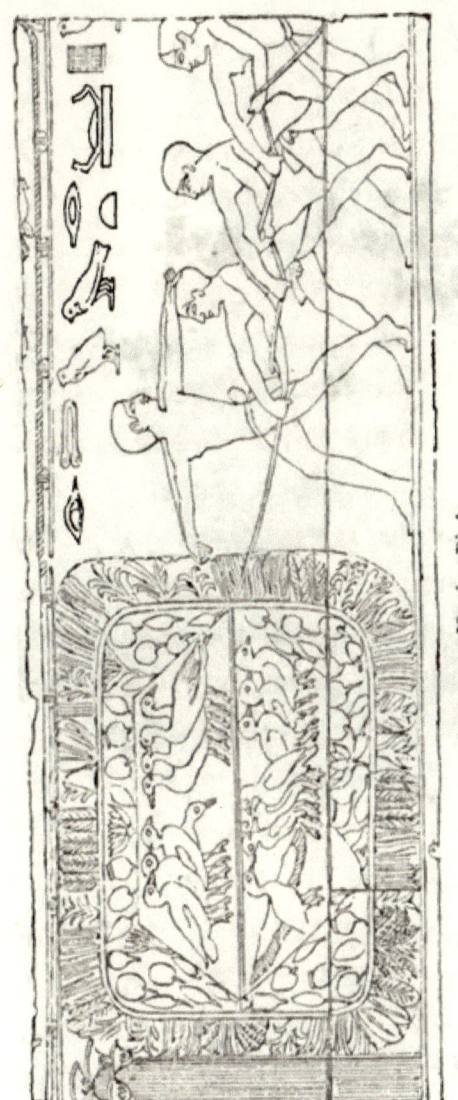

Netting Birds.

upon the sand, marks of the footprints left there by the bearers of the coffin.

Here we seem brought face to face with a very remote past. All is so strangely distant and unlike, but at the same time all is strangely near and like ourselves and our own life to-day. Here, *e.g.*, is the entrance-passage to the tomb of Nefer-mat, a high officer of state and 'friend of the king,' who married Atet, a royal princess. On one side of the passage we see Nefer-mat, with his wife clinging to his arm; on the other he is represented with his little son at his feet. In front of us the husband and wife are again delineated; her long hair falls loosely over her shoulders, and she places her hand upon her heart in token of devoted affection.

Atet appears to have survived her husband, and her own tomb is close at hand. Amongst the scenes depicted there is one in which Nefer-mat is employed in netting fowl; the wife is seated near, watching the sport, and servants are bringing her the game. The hieroglyphic inscription says: 'Princess Atet receives with pleasure the game caught by the chief noble, Nefer-mat.'

In another of these tombs were discovered the wonderful statues of Ra-hotep and his beautiful wife Nefert, which are now in the museum at Boulak. Ra-hotep was a prince, very likely a son of Senefru, who died young; he was a captain in the army, and chief priest of Ra, at On. These, the most ancient known statues in the world, are 'marvels of life-like reality.' The Egyptians always excelled in portrait sculpture; the figures may be stiff and ill-drawn, but the faces are beyond doubt truthful and characteristic likenesses. Men of learning were held in honour at the court of these early Pharaohs, as well as architects and sculptors. But the literature of those days may be said to have perished. Portions of it, enshrined in the sacred writings, have survived, and there is, besides, one venerable manuscript of the time of the fifth dynasty, which has come down to us. It is called the *Maxims of Ptah-hotep* and is the oldest manuscript known. The writer was a prince by birth, and a governor; he lived to be more than a hundred years old, and after a long and varied experience of life, when the infirmities of old age had come upon him, he recorded, for the use and benefit of all, the teaching of that serene and simple wisdom which is never new and never old—such as the following :—

'A good son is the gift of God.'

'If thou art a wise man, bring up thy son in the love of God.'

'If any one bears himself proudly, he will be humbled by God, who gave his strength.'

'If thou hast become great after having been lowly, and art the first in thy town; if thou art known for thy wealth, and art become a great lord—let not thy heart grow proud because of thy riches, for it is God who was the author of them for thee. Despise not another who may be as thou once wast; be towards him as towards thine equal.'

'With the courage that knowledge gives, discuss with the ignorant as with the learned. Good words shine more than the emerald, which the hand of the slave finds on the pebbles.'

'He who obeys not does really nothing; he sees knowledge in ignorance, virtue in vices; he commits daily and boldly all sort of crimes, and lives as if he was dead. What others know to be death, is his daily life.'

'God lives through all that is good and pure.'

And he concludes :—

'Thus shalt thou obtain health of body and the favour of the king, and pass the years of thy life without falsehood. I am become one of the ancients of the earth. I have passed 110 years of life—fulfilling my duty to the king, and I have continued to stand in his favour.'

The venerable Ptah-hotep was buried in one of the tombs that are grouped around the ancient pyramid of Sakkara. Near his burial-place is the vast tomb of Thi, on which is recorded, in sculptured story, the course of his daily life. Of his own birth and parentage nothing is said, but he so distinguished himself that the king gave him his daughter in marriage. Thi was royal scribe, president of royal writings, and conductor of the king's works. His tomb must indeed have been the work of a lifetime. We see him there, amidst the scenes of rural life, watching over the ingathering of the harvest, or fowling in the marshes; one while he is listening to the strains of music, another time he is steering his little vessel on the broad waters of the Nile. Servant girls are carrying on their heads and in their hands, in baskets or in jars, the produce of his estates—wine, bread, geese, pigeons, fruit, and flowers. Above is depicted a humorous scene, such as Egyptian artists delighted in. A number of donkeys pass in file, their saddle-cloths are ornamented with fringes, and they are laden with panniers of grain. Men walk by the side to steady the heavy loads. One load, however, has shifted from its place, and two men are trying to put it back; the animal is restive, and one man has hold of him by the tail while another has grasped his nose. The donkey coming immediately behind has seized the opportunity of the halt to give the man in front of him a poke with his nose. Each driver is armed with a stout stick, and one of them is just raising his against the unruly animal. It is evident that donkeys were considered troublesome and obstinate some four or five thousand years ago, that their humours amused the Egyptian artists, and that donkey drivers then, as now, were ready to use their sticks.

In another drawing Thi is seen in a boat made of reeds, superintending a hippopotamus hunt. One of his men has succeeded in getting a rope round the neck of one savage-looking beast, and is preparing to despatch him with a long club. The river is full of fish, and one of the hippopotami has just seized a little crocodile between his enormous jaws. In another picture a crocodile hunt is represented, whilst in one drawing we see an angler who is evidently out for a day's sport in one of the small reed boats. He is in the act of drawing a fish out of the water, and by his side he has loaves of bread, a cup, and a bottle.

Nowhere is depicted a scene of battle or warlike display, everything speaks of rural and domestic life.

But we do not see the great men of Pharaoh's court only in the scenes and amusements of life. Funeral rites are also represented. The body is seen embalmed and carried to its last resting-place; funeral gifts are offered in rich abundance. No obligation was more sacred than that of bringing funeral oblations and offering prayer for the departed parent or friend. Inscriptions over the tombs called even on the passer-by to stay a while and offer up the customary invocation. The form of this invocation varied from age to age, but the main burden of its petitions was that Osiris would 'grant the funeral oblations of all good things; that the departed one might not be repulsed at the entrance of the unseen world, but might be glorified amongst the blessed ones in presence of the Good Being, that he (or she) might breathe the delicious breezes of the north wind, and drink from the depth of the river.'

It was customary to build a chamber at the entrance to the tomb, in which the family and friends of the departed assembled from time to time to offer oblations and prayers, and to realise the actual presence of those who were gone. The walls of these rooms were covered with pictured and sculptured scenes taken from the varied scenes of daily life. They were adorned 'as for a home of pleasure and joy'—no thought of gloom is even suggested.

The names given to the pyramids by their royal builders are very striking in this respect. Amongst them we find the 'Abode of Life,' the 'Refreshing Place,' the 'Good Rising,' the 'Most Holy,' 'Most Lovely,' or 'Most Abiding Place,' the 'Rising of the Soul.'

The earliest of the pyramids were unsculptured and unadorned within, so there was attached to each of them a small sanctuary or memorial chapel; the office of 'priest of the royal pyramid' being held in high estimation and conferred on the most illustrious men of the day.

During their lifetime the Pharaohs were regarded by their people as representatives of the gods, or even as emanations from the Divine Being. After their death their memory was preserved and sacred rites were performed by the priests attached to their respective pyramids. Down to the latest days of the Empire, and even in the reign of the Ptolemies (three or four thousand years after they had been laid to rest 'each within his own house'), priests were still officiating in memory of Khufu, Khafra, or Senefru—the far-famed pyramid builders.

For whilst the names of some amongst the later Pharaohs are emblazoned on the page of history as conquerors of high renown, who founded an Egyptian empire and gathered in rich and varied tribute from many subject races—those ancient monarchs are known and will ever be remembered as the kings 'who built the pyramids.'

CHAPTER IV.

Civil War and Break-up of the Kingdom— Reunion and Recovery.

THE last sovereign of the sixth dynasty was a queen named Nitocris. After her death occurs a perfect blank in Egyptian history. Not a line of hieroglyphic writing, not a fragment of a ruin has survived from this period of darkness and silence. Of the seventh dynasty the very names are lost; of the eighth, nothing but the names has been preserved. The names, however, are so similar to those of the sixth dynasty, that we may conclude that these rulers were of the same royal line and descendants of Mena.

It may be gathered from the bare fact of the accession of a female sovereign that the direct male line had failed. Nitocris appears to have left no children, and it is easy to imagine how rival claims and dissension would arise; each claimant asserting his right as next of kin, to wear the double crown.

But at the same time the double crown lost much of its splendour. Other pretenders started up, ambitious men, claiming no right of kinship certainly, but anxious to make their own profit during this period of discord and weakness in the ruling house. Egypt was divided into forty-two districts or 'nomes,' and each of these possessed its own governor (*hak*, or prince, he was called) and each was to some extent a government complete within itself. The office of these prince-governors was often hereditary, and there was always a danger lest some powerful and popular governor should aim at setting up a petty kingdom of his own, in the event of the ruling hand becoming enfeebled. During a female reign the controlling power would be lessened, whilst the prospect of a disputed succession was awakening ambitious hopes and schemes. So long as Nitocris lived, the reverence due to a direct representative of the Pharaohs might prove some restraint, but at her death the smouldering ambitions and rivalries of scions of the royal house and of powerful provincial governors could hardly fail to burst forth, and find vent in fierce flames of discord and of civil war.

Would we form to ourselves some idea of the state of Egypt during the ensuing centuries, we must picture a feeble scion of the ancient line ruling at Memphis over a territory barely extending beyond the capital; for in the north the foreign races would seize their opportunity for invading and encroaching upon the rich Delta land, thus blocking the great highway by the river; and farther south a rival dynasty is established at Heracleopolis, in Middle Egypt, not to reckon the other petty kingdoms or principalities into which the country is broken up—the whole a scene of ceaseless jealousies and mutual conflict.

At length in the extreme south certain kinglike figures emerge of a more commanding appearance, and seen by a clearer light. The Antefs first, a family of ancient and illustrious, though not royal descent, who had set up their dominion at a town then insignificant and unknown to fame—Thebes. The burial-places of the kings of this family (who are sometimes reckoned in the eleventh dynasty) have been discovered in Western Thebes. Their tombs are plain, and but little ornamented; there are some brick pyramids of no great size, and some fragments of small broken obelisks. In one of the memorial chambers is depicted an Antef who assumed the title of the 'Great;' he appears to have been a sportsman, and is to be seen surrounded by his dogs, each of which is distinguished by its name. From the days of these kings a literary relic also has come down to us. The 'festal dirge' of the Egyptians bears the name of the *Song of the House of King Antef*. Many, many ages later, Herodotus, travelling in Egypt, told of the custom which prevailed of carrying round during an entertainment a figure representing a mummy, whilst the bearer repeated the words: 'Cast your eyes upon this figure; after death you yourself will resemble it; eat, drink, then, and be happy;' words plainly recalling the 'solemn festal dirge' which dated back to the 'House of Antef,' about 2000 years before his time, and which was to the following effect:—

'All hail the good Prince, the worthy man who has

passed away! Behold the end! the end of those who possess houses and of those who have them not. I have heard the sayings of the wise:—"What is prosperity? All passes as though it had not been—no man returneth thence to tell us what they say or do."

'Fulfil, then, thy desire, O man, whilst yet thou livest. Anoint thine head with oil, and clothe thee in fine linen adorned with gold—Make use of God's good gifts.

'For the day will come for thee also when voices are heard no more; he who is at rest heareth not the cry of those who mourn. No mourning may deliver him that is within the tomb.

'Feast, then, in peace—for none can carry away his goods with him, nor can he who goeth hence return again.'

There are, then, a few scanty records left of the Antef family and their rule in the south. Still more distinct and commanding are the figures of another family, the brave and warlike Mentuhoteps; who eventually succeeded in restoring order over a considerable portion of the distracted and divided land. This family was of Theban origin, and the centre of their government was in that city, then so obscure, though destined to become in after days the crown of ancient cities and the wonder of the ancient world—'hundred-gated Thebes.'

With wise forethought the Mentuhoteps devoted their attention to the development of trade and industry in the south. The passage of the great water-way of the Nile was impeded, but there was an outlet for commerce by a route leading eastward from the Nile to the Red Sea. Koptos, a town not far north of Thebes, stood at the entrance of the desert rocky valley of Hammamat, through which merchantmen and travellers made a weary and painful eight days' journey to the Red Sea. The Mentuhotep kings themselves took up their residence sometimes at Koptos, and the gloomy valley of Hammamat gradually became a scene of busy industry. Mines of gold and silver ore were worked there, and stone was hewn from its quarries for building purposes at Thebes, which was continually growing in extent and in importance. For the benefit of the labourers in the hot valley, and for the refreshment of travellers and their beasts, a deep well, ten cubits broad, was sunk by royal order. The whole district was placed under the special guardianship of the god Khem, who was known as the 'Protecting Lord of the mountain.' The rocks near Koptos are to this day covered with inscriptions—the invocations and prayers of many generations, both of workmen and of wayfarers. The development of trade and industry brought an increase both of wealth and power to the Mentuhoteps and their people. During the reign of the last sovereign of the eleventh dynasty, a more distant expedition was undertaken.

The land of Punt[1] was well known by name and repute to the Egyptians; they regarded it as a sacred region (*Ta-neter*, the 'holy land'), and it was known to be a hilly country, whose shores were washed by the Red Sea, and to be celebrated for many rare and precious products; for choice and costly woods; for gems and frankincense, and fragrant spices; for trees and plants unknown at home; for birds of strange plumage, giraffes, monkeys, and leopards. King Sankhkara despatched an expedition thither under the command of a nobleman named Hanno. Hanno tells us the story himself: 'I was sent,' he says, 'to conduct ships to

---

[1] It is not quite certain whether Punt was on the Arabian or Abyssinian shore of the Red Sea, probably the latter.

the land of Punt, to fetch for the king sweet-smelling spices.' He started with 3000 men, well armed and carefully provided with water, which was carried in skins on poles. Through the valley of Hammamat he pressed on rapidly to the sea; there he embarked, after offering up rich sacrifices. 'I brought back,' he says, 'all kinds of products, and I brought back precious stones for the statues of the temples.'

The route between Koptos and the Red Sea continued to be a highway for commerce down to the days of the Greeks and Romans.

CHAPTER V.

Twelfth Dynasty—'Instructions' of Amenemhat I.—Story of Saneha.

THERE was a certain unity in Egyptian worships, but in various localities the chief deities bore different names, and were regarded under varying aspects. The worship of some of these chief deities, however, became general, if not universal, at a very early period; *e.g.* that of Osiris, Isis, and Horus, the triad of Abydos; that of Ra and Tum,[1] chief gods of On, and that of Ptah, the centre of which was Memphis. The Thebaid—*i.e.* the district surrounding Thebes—had its own local divinities also. Khem, 'Lord of the mountain,' was adored at Koptos; Amen (worshipped in connection with Mut, the 'Divine Mother,' and

---

[1] Tum, symbolised in the setting, Ra, in the risen sun, appear to signify respectively the hidden and the manifested deity—closely corresponding with Osiris—Horus; for there is a unity underlying the apparently endless varieties of Egyptian worships.

Khons) was the chief god of Thebes. He was destined to become, under the name of Amen-Ra, the chief amongst Egyptian gods at a later day.

The name of the first sovereign of the twelfth dynasty, Amenemhat ('Amen the leader'), bespeaks its southern origin. This great monarch followed up the successes of the Mentuhoteps, and finally re-united Egypt under one sceptre, although at the cost of many years of severe conflict. Then he had to drive back the Kushites, who had encroached on the south, and the Libyans and the Amu, who troubled the northern borders; and after he had restored the ancient boundaries there was still need of perpetual vigilance upon the frontiers. On the north-east, where lay the greatest danger, he erected fortresses and built a strong wall of defence.

But although Amenemhat I. had been able to restore the ancient boundaries of Egypt, and all the country was subject, nominally, to his sway, it is certain that the kinglets and chieftains whom he had reduced bore him but little affection, and yielded only a sullen and constrained obedience; in fact there is evidence of a hatred so vindictive that it did not scruple to resort even to the dagger of midnight assassination. But King Amenemhat did not rest content with the supremacy he had won; he strove, and not without success in the end, to win the goodwill and affection of the people, and he bequeathed to his successors a legacy of peace and prosperity that lasted for many generations. In the 'Instructions' which he left for his son Usertesen (whom he had associated with him on the throne), we may see both the high ideal this great and wise sovereign had formed of his own duties, and also form some idea of the perils and anxieties amidst which he strove to perform them.

'Now thou art king,' he says to his son; 'strive to excel those who have gone before thee. Keep peace between thy people and thyself, lest they should be afraid of thee. Go amongst them, keep not thyself aloof; do not let it be only great lords and nobles whom thou takest to thy heart as brothers; nevertheless, let none come near thee whose friendship thou hast not proved.

'Let thine own heart be strong, for know this, O man, that in the day of adversity thy servants' help will fail thee. As for me, I have given to the lowly and I have strengthened the weak. I have breathed courage into hearts where there was none.

'Thee have I exalted from being a subject, and I have upheld thee, that men may fear before thee. I have adorned myself with fine linen, so that I was like the pure water flowers; I anointed myself with fragrant oil, as though it had been water.

'My remembrance lives in men's hearts because I caused the sorrow of the afflicted to cease; their cry was no longer heard. The conflicts are over, though they had been renewed again and again, for the land had become like a mighty one who is forgetful of the past. Neither the ignorant nor the learned man was able to endure.[1]

' 'Once after supper, when the shades of night had fallen, I went to seek repose. I lay down and stretched myself upon the carpets of my

---

[1] Words very suggestive as to the distractions and warfare of the preceding centuries, when the land had indeed seemed to have 'forgotten the past.'

house; my soul began to seek after sleep. But lo! armed men had assembled to attack me; I was helpless as the torpid snake in the field. Then I aroused myself, and collected all my strength, but it was to strike at a foe who made no stand. If I encountered an armed rebel I made the coward turn and fly; not even in the darkness was he brave; no one fought.

'Nor was there ever a time of need that found me unprepared. And when the day of my passing hence came, and I knew it not —I had never given ear to the courtiers who desired me to abdicate in thy favour. I sat ever by thy side, and planned all things for thee.

'I never neglected anything that was for the benefit of my servants. If locusts came arrayed for plunder, if conspiracy assailed me at home, if the Nile was low, and the wells were dry; if my enemies took advantage of thy youth to conspire to do ill,—I never faltered from the day that I was born. Never was the like seen since the days of the heroes.

'My messengers have travelled to the south and to the north. I stood upon the frontiers to keep watch. I stationed men armed with scimitars upon the boundaries, and I was armed with a scimitar myself.

'I grew abundance of corn, and the god of corn gave me the rising of the Nile over the cultivated land. None was hungry through me, none thirsted through me; every one took heed to obey my words. All my orders increased the affection my people had for me.

'I hunted the lion, and brought home the crocodile. I fought the Nubians, and took the Libyans captive. I turned my forces against the Sati; he fawned upon me like a dog.

'I built myself a house[1] adorned with gold; its ceiling was of azure, its galleries of stone. It was made for eternity. I possess the everlasting powers of the gods. There are many secret passages therein; I alone possess the key. None knows the way but thee, O Usertesen. Thou enterest, and thou wilt see me with thine eyes amongst the spirits who do thee honour.

'All I have done is for thee. Do thou place upon my statue the double crown and

---

[1] I am inclined to think that this 'house' and its secret passages meant his tomb, whither his son would resort to invoke his father's memory, who, in the 'boat of Ra,' would not forget Usertesen.

the tokens of divinity; let the seal of friendship unite us. In the boat of Ra am I offering prayers for thee. It was my power that raised thee to the throne and upheld thee there.'

The latter years of Amenemhat's reign flowed tranquilly by. 'The land had rest' from the warfare of centuries; and the sovereigns applied themselves to restoring the temples of the gods which had been neglected during the troublous times through which Egypt had passed. Amenemhat laid the foundation of the Great Temple at Thebes, whose colossal ruins still excite the wonder of the traveller at Karnak.

During the joint reign of these two sovereigns peace and confidence were so far restored that it was possible to deal generously with fugitives and exiles. A kindly answer was accordingly sent to a humble petition from one of these, Saneha by name, who had fled or been banished the country many years before. He has left an account of his experiences, which has fortunately come down to us. The first lines are wanting that would have given the events which led to his hurried flight; but it is not difficult to imagine how a young and powerful noble might have become compromised in insurrection or conspiracy during the earlier years of Amenemhat's reign—so gravely compromised that his recall and friendly reception by the kings was regarded with suspicion and disapproval by some of the royal family themselves. The narrative opens thus—'When I was about to set out, my heart was troubled, my hands trembled, numbness fell on my limbs. I disguised myself as a seller of herbs;[1] twice I started and turned back . . . I passed the night in a garden; when it was day I arose, and by supper-time had arrived at the town. . . . There I embarked on a barge without a rudder, and came to Abu; the rest of the journey I made on foot. I came to the fortress which the king built to keep off the Sakti, and I was received by an old man, a seller of herbs. But I was afraid when I beheld the watchmen upon the walls relieving each other daily. In the dawn I proceeded,

---

[1] Or 'I hid among the shrubs.' There is often considerable uncertainty in rendering the phrases of such ancient narratives as the 'Story of Saneha.'

and went on my journey from place to place. Thirst overtook me, and my throat was parched; it was as the taste of death. But I encouraged myself, and my limbs waxed strong, for I heard the pleasant voice of cattle. I saw a Sakti. He spoke to me, saying, "O thou that art from Egypt! whither art thou going?" Then he gave me water, and poured out milk for me. He brought me to his people, and they conducted me from place to place till we came to Tennu. The king said, "Remain with me; here thou wilt hear the language of Egypt." I told him what had happened; he understood my condition, and heard the story of my disgrace. Then he questioned me, saying, "Why hast thou done these things? . . . And is it true that the wealth of the house of Amenemhat reacheth unto heaven?" And I said, "It is certain."'

Saneha then tells the king of his earlier life; he extols the fame of king Amenemhat and the martial prowess and great popularity of his son —to which the king answers, 'Yea, Egypt is safe—it is well. Behold, so long as thou art with me, I will do thee good.' And he kept his word, giving the Egyptian exile lands and possessions and marrying him to his eldest daughter. For many years Saneha dwelt in the strange country, and saw his children grow up around him. Nor was he unmindful of his own past sufferings, but was ever ready to 'give water to the thirsty and set the wanderer in the way.' He aided the king also against his enemies, so that, 'beholding the valour of his arm,' he made him chief amongst his children. Presently Saneha receives a challenge from a certain strong man, hitherto undisputed champion of the Tennu. The prospect of this single combat excited intense interest. All Tennu assembled to behold it, and 'every heart was sorry for Saneha,' who was to encounter so redoubtable a foe. But of course Saneha triumphs, and obtains possession of his enemy's person and goods. 'I got great treasure and wealth, I got much cattle.'

In spite of riches and renown and royal favour, the heart of the exile grows sad; old age is at hand, and an irrepressible longing after home and native land seizes upon him. He ventures to approach the all-powerful King of Egypt with a humble petition for pardon and recall. 'Let me be buried,' he says, 'in the place where I was born.' His petition was most graciously received. Usertesen sent a messenger to the land of the Tennu, laden with many royal gifts and intrusted with a mandate drawn up in his father's name. 'Thou hast passed through the lands,' writes the king, 'going from country to country as thy heart bade thee. Behold what thou hast done thou hast done. Thou shalt not be called to account for what thou hast said in the assembly of young men, nor for the business that thou didst devise. If thou comest to Egypt, a house shall be prepared for thee. If thou dost homage to Pharaoh, thou shalt be numbered amongst the king's councillors. . . . Lo, thou hast arrived at middle age; thou hast passed the flower of thy youth. Think upon the day of burial, upon the passage to Amenti.[1] Cedar oil and wrappings shall be given thee—service shall be done to thee in the day of thy burial. At the door of thy tomb the poor shall make supplication; invocations shall be made before thee.'

---

[1] The unseen or hidden world.

This letter reached Saneha as he was in the midst of his people. Overcome with emotion he prostrated himself upon the ground. He first caused the mandate to be read aloud before his chosen men, and then assembled his household to hear the news, 'I being myself like one mad.' Without delay Saneha sent his answer, worded with the profoundest humility and gratitude, anxious only that the king's majesty should not hold the people of Tennu responsible as though they had in any way been concerned in his guilt or had aided his flight.

Saneha immediately arranged everything for his departure; he set his eldest son in his place, and appointed a director over his workmen. Then he bade adieu to the friendly people among whom he had so long sojourned, and they assembled in crowds to wish him a good journey and happy arrival at court. When he reached the country he had left by stealth, slinking away in disguise like a thief, he was met by princes of the royal family, who conducted him forthwith into the presence of the king. 'I found his majesty in the old place, in the pavilion of pure gold. I fell upon my face, as one amazed. The "god" addressed me mildly, but I was as one brought out of the dark; my tongue was dumb, my limbs failed me, I knew not whether I was alive or dead. His majesty said to one of the councillors, "Lift him up that I may speak to him." His majesty said, "Behold, thou hast gone about the lands like a runaway. Now old age has come upon thee. Thy renown is not small; be not silent and without words, for thy name is famous." Saneha replies in broken utterances; 'Behold, oh, my lord, how can I answer these things? Is not God's hand upon me; it is terrible. There is that within me that causeth pain. I am before thee. Thou art mighty. Let thy majesty do as it pleaseth thee.' The royal family were now admitted, and the king said to the queen, ' Behold Saneha; he went away as an Amu; he has become a Sakti.'[1] To add to the confusion and alarm of the repentant exile, there now arises a great cry from some of the princes of the royal family itself, who exclaim with one voice—' He is not

[1] Foreign tribes on north-east frontier. The point is lost for us.

in the right, O my lord the king!' But Amenemhat, as we know, was not one to be thwarted or turned aside from his purpose;[1] and he only replies, 'He is in the right,' and proceeds forthwith to lavish tokens of reconciliation and favour upon Saneha. He gives him precedence in the palace, and appoints him one of the king's intimate councillors. He is clothed in fine linen, the attire of a prince, and is anointed with fragrant oil. A princely habitation is assigned for his use whilst the labourers are busily employed erecting for him a house 'befitting a councillor.' No sooner is it completed than Saneha's thoughts turn to that other house which he must prepare for himself in the western land—to the day of burial and the 'passage to Amenti' of which the royal letter had spoken. He built himself a tomb of stone. The king selected the spot, the chief painter designed and the sculptors carved it; all the decorations were of hewn stone. The field in which it was situated was made over to him as his own possession, and he adds: 'My image was

---

[1] At least he says of himself in his Instructions, 'I never faltered since the day I was born.'

engraved upon the portal in pure gold. His majesty commanded it to be done. I was in favour with the king until the day of his death came.'

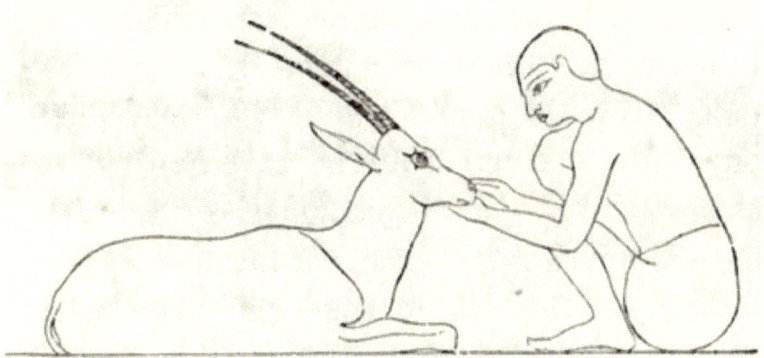

Caressing a Gazelle.

CHAPTER VI.

Successors of Amenemhat I.—Two Provinces added to Egypt.

THE stone for the sarcophagus of King Amenemhat I. was hewn in the valley of Hammamat, and he was laid to rest in his pyramid called *Kha-nefer*, the 'Beautiful Rising,' leaving behind him an honoured name and an inheritance of peaceful days. Usertesen I., his son and successor, reigned in profound tranquillity, and turned his attention to the temples of the gods, which were neglected and falling into decay. They were, he said, the only monuments that could truly confer immortality on a king. First of all, he called together an assembly of the chief men of the land in that ancient home of Egyptian wisdom and learning, the City of the Sun, to consult about a temple that should be raised, 'worthy of the name of Ra.' Usertesen himself laid the foundation-stone, and gave the directions for the carrying out of the work. The ruins of both temple and city are now buried deep beneath the soil, but of the two stately obelisks of rose-coloured granite, which stood at the gateway of the temple, one is still standing in solitary grandeur amid the quiet fields; the hieroglyphs upon its surface still record that 'the Ruler of the North and South, Lord of the Two Countries, Son of the Sun, Usertesen—beloved of the Gods of On, living for ever, the good god,' executed this work.

At the ancient sanctuary of Abydos a temple was erected to Osiris, and Memphis was not overlooked. But whilst duly careful for those time-honoured sanctuaries, Usertesen did not neglect the new southern capital, and he carried on the construction of the great temple of Amen, which his father Amenemhat had begun.

The frontiers were vigilantly guarded, and now that quiet times had come back the mines in the Sinaitic peninsula were re-opened and worked. A thousand years had passed since they were first explored at the command of Senefru, and his name had become venerable in its antiquity throughout that region, where he was worshipped as a guardian deity, together with the goddess Hathor, protectress of the district.

One warlike expedition was undertaken during this reign, for the purpose of fixing the boundary to the south and of bringing back gold from Nubia. The command was intrusted to one Ameni, who has left a brief record of the expedition. The king's eldest son accompanied him, and his success was certainly remarkable, if his statement is true, that of the 400 men he took with him not one was missing when he returned with the golden spoil. This Ameni was the head of that illustrious family, whose tombs at Beni-Hassan have proved such an invaluable storehouse for the investigator. They were hereditary governors of the district, or nome, and their power was very great. Under the firm controlling hand of the sovereigns of this great dynasty, the power and ambition of the prince-governors, which had once split up and half ruined Egypt, were turned into nobler channels, and sought after more peaceful honours. The *Maxims of*

Amenemhat I. seem to awaken a response and to find an echo in the memorials left by some of the powerful governors, who were now serving loyally under the crown. Ameni, who gives an account of his warlike doings in the south, also tells us that he was a 'kind master and gentle of heart, a governor who loved his city.' He ruled for many years in his district of Mah, and he says: 'I kept back nothing for myself; no little child was vexed through me; no widow was afflicted. I never interfered with the fisherman or troubled the shepherd. There was neither famine nor hunger in my days. I diligently cultivated every field in my district, from the north to the south, to its utmost extent, so that there was food enough for all. I gave to the widow as to the married woman, and I never showed favour to the great above the lowly.'

King and noble may alike have fallen short of their ideal, but at any rate their standard was high, and their words recall those of the departed spirit, who had to declare before Osiris in the judgment-hall of Truth—'I have not oppressed the miserable; I have not imposed work beyond his power on any officer; I have allowed no master to maltreat his slave; I have caused none to weep or to perish with hunger. I have neither blasphemed the king nor my father, nor have I mocked or despised God in my heart. I have given bread to the hungry, water to him that was athirst, clothes to the naked, and shelter to the wanderer.' There is a beautiful eulogy somewhere recorded on an Egyptian tomb—' His love was the food of the poor, the blessing of the weak, the riches of him who had nothing.'

Egypt was probably never more prosperous, nor her people happier, than during the centuries in which the Amenemhats and Usertesens ruled the land. The only reign in which serious warfare occurred was that of Usertesen III. He determined to acquire for Egypt the disputed territory in the south—*Ta-Khent* (Nubia) —and, with it, its golden treasures. But he did not succeed in finally conquering and driving back the dark-hued tribes until after a very fierce and protracted struggle. He erected fortresses on the southern frontier, and an inscription on the rock proclaimed: 'This

BOATMEN AND CATTLE DRIVERS.

is the southern boundary, fixed in the eighth year of King Usertesen III. No negro shall be permitted to pass it except for the purpose of bringing vessels laden with their asses, camels, and goats, or of trading by barter in Ta-Khent. To such negroes, on the contrary, every favour shall be shown.'

If Usertesen III. secured one new province for Egypt by the ruthless force of war, his successor, Amenemhat III., won another by gentler means.

Egypt is, no doubt, what Herodotus called it, the 'gift' of the Nile. But for the Nile the burning wastes of Sahara would stretch eastwards without interruption to the Red Sea. By means of the great river and its yearly inundation, the long narrow valley between the Libyan and the Arabian mountains is watered and richly fertilised for the space of several miles; where the inundation ceases the desert sand begins. This long strip of fertile country, together with the Delta into which it expands, constituted Egypt;[1] *Khemi* (the black country),

---

[1] Egypt is the name given to the country by the Greeks, and is of very uncertain derivation.

its people called it from the dark colour of its rich soil, which rewarded the husbandman's toil with two or three crops a year—crops of a luxuriance difficult for us to realise. The name of Egypt was a synonym for rich fertility: 'Well watered everywhere,' we read in Genesis, 'like the garden of the Lord, like the land of Egypt.'

In the days when the twelfth dynasty ruled, *i.e.* probably more than 2000 B.C., the average rise of the Nile was more than twenty feet higher than it is at the present day. At the point where Usertesen III. had erected his frontier fortress, the height attained by the river during many successive inundations is recorded. His successor, Amenemhat III., not only carefully noted the annual rise, but turned his attention to the great work of controlling the overflow, for the country was liable to suffer severely in case either of an excess or a deficiency.

Westward from the Nile, behind the Libyan hills, lies the valley of Fayoum, about 60 miles distant from Cairo. There the king ordered the excavation of that immense basin or artificial sea known to us as Lake Mœris, and caused it to be connected by canals with the river. Lake Mœris was about 30 miles in circumference, and here the surplus waters were stored, to be distributed by irrigation or withheld, as might be best. The rock-encircled and desolate Fayoum thus became a smiling oasis, full of the most luxuriant vegetation, and alive with busy industry. When the Greek Herodotus visited Egypt, some 2000 years later, Lake Mœris was still in existence, as were also the two pyramids that stood either on its banks or in its centre. A still greater wonder met the eye of the inquiring traveller, and excited his profoundest amazement. This was the vast structure close by Lake Mœris, which the Greeks called the Labyrinth, for what reason it is hard to say. Herodotus tells us of this other gigantic work of Amenemhat III., that it had twelve courts, with gates opposite each other, and that it contained 3000 chambers, half of which were above and half below ground; the courts were adorned with columns, and the walls covered with inscriptions. This colossal edifice covered a space 1150 feet in length, and 850 in breadth; its purpose is not altogether clear, but there seems some reason to think that it may have been intended for a vast Hall of

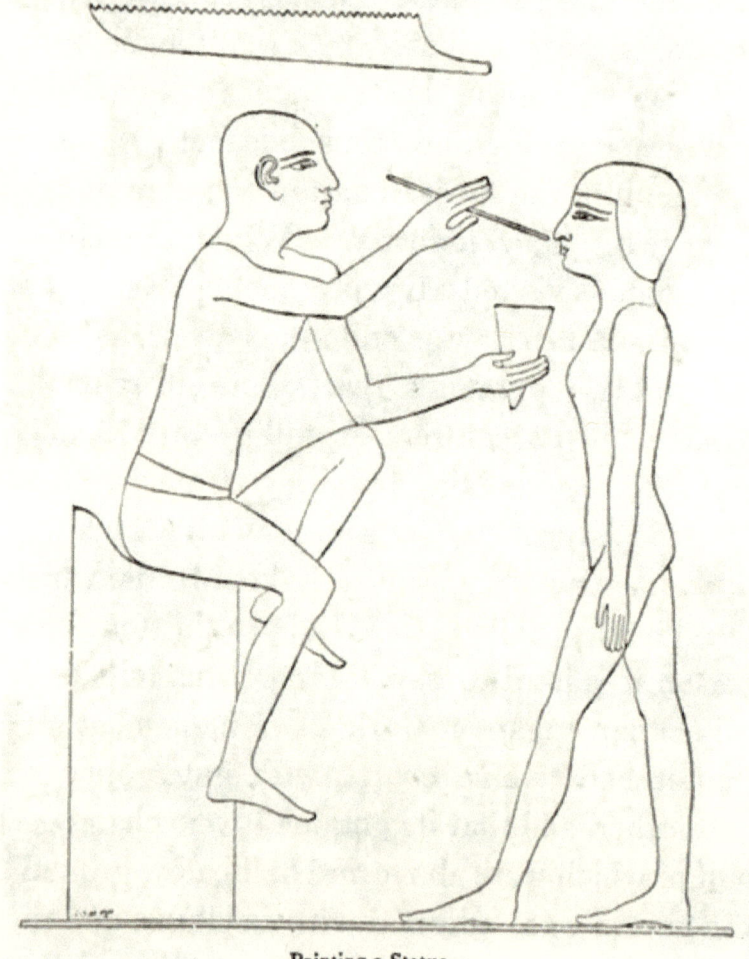

Painting a Statue.

Assembly. It is all in ruins now. Lepsius, who in 1844 visited the district, which is miles distant from the Nile, states that it had been so arranged that three enormous masses of buildings enclosed a square place 600 feet

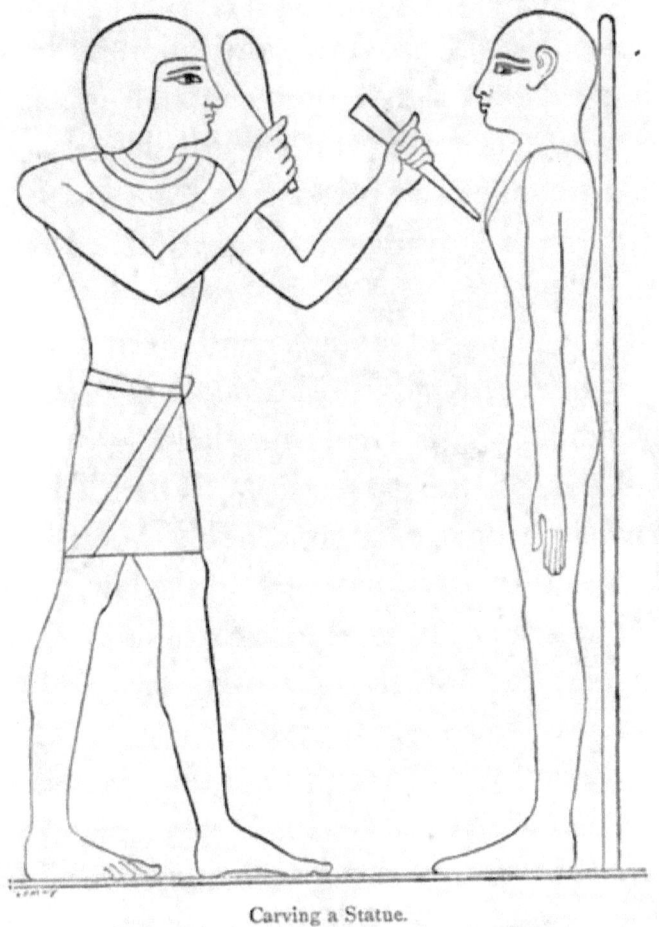

Carving a Statue.

long by 500 broad, and that in this square once stood the courts and columns mentioned by

Herodotus, mighty fragments of which the explorer dug up: upon them was carved the name of the royal builder, Amenemhat III.

After this peaceful victory, which won for Egypt so fair a province, and adorned it with such marvels of art, there is not much left to record concerning the twelfth dynasty. Its annals are quiet and prosperous throughout, and its art was progressive and beautiful. No man in the kingdom was more honoured than the artist, the man 'of enlightened spirit and skilfully working hand.' The office of 'architect to Pharaoh'[1] was sometimes held by sons and grandsons of the sovereign. There is a remarkable account of a great noble, Mentuhotep, who was a judge and learned in the law, a priest and a warrior. It is recorded of him that, as chief architect of the king, he promoted the worship of the gods, and instructed the inhabitants of the country according to the best of his knowledge, as God had commanded to be done. He protected the unfortunate, and freed him that was in need of freedom. 'Peace was

[1] Pharaoh is derived from the words *Per-aa*, 'Great House,' and answers pretty nearly to the 'Sublime Porte' at Constantinople. Later on it is used as the sovereign's name.

in the utterances of his mouth, and the learning of the wise Thoth [1] was on his tongue. Very skilful in artistic work, with his own hand he carried out his designs as they ought to be done.'

The beautiful rock-hewn caves of Beni-Hassan bear witness to the rare excellence attained by architecture and sculpture. These tombs and memorial chambers were excavated in a limestone cliff on the east bank of the Nile, 160 miles south of Cairo. They were for generations the burial-place of the illustrious family of the Khnumhoteps, descendants of Ameni (p. 66), and hereditary governors of the district. The roofs of these rock tombs are vaulted; at the entrance to the northernmost, where Ameni, head of the family lay, are columns of great beauty, so closely resembling those called Doric 2000 years later that it is difficult not to believe that they served as prototypes. At the entrance to another tomb are columns still more graceful in design; these are purely

---

[1] This god, symbolised in the moon, was more especially the god of knowledge and science. He was the inventor of all arts, and the inspirer of the sacred writings, the lawgiver, and the advocate and justifier of the good before the tribunal of Osiris.

Egyptian in style, and are formed of slender reeds bound together, and expanding into capitals like papyrus or lotus buds or flowers. Here was buried Khnumhotep, grandson of Ameni, a man of high character and great renown. The walls of the interior are covered with pictorial representations, invaluable for the insight they afford into the daily life of those long past times. Amongst the scenes depicted on the walls of Khnumhotep's funeral chamber is one of much significance. A family group, consisting of 37 persons, is ushered into the presence of the great Egyptian lord, who receives them standing and surrounded by his dogs. They are Amu—foreigners of the East—and their errand is to bring from the land of Pitshu (Midian) a certain mineral substance from which was prepared a paint for the eyes much used in Egypt. Their faces are wholly unlike the Egyptians; they have aquiline noses and long black beards. They are evidently immigrants come to settle in the land. The men are armed, the women gaily dressed. They bring with them presents—the ibis and gazelle, and the splendid wild goat of the Sinai desert;

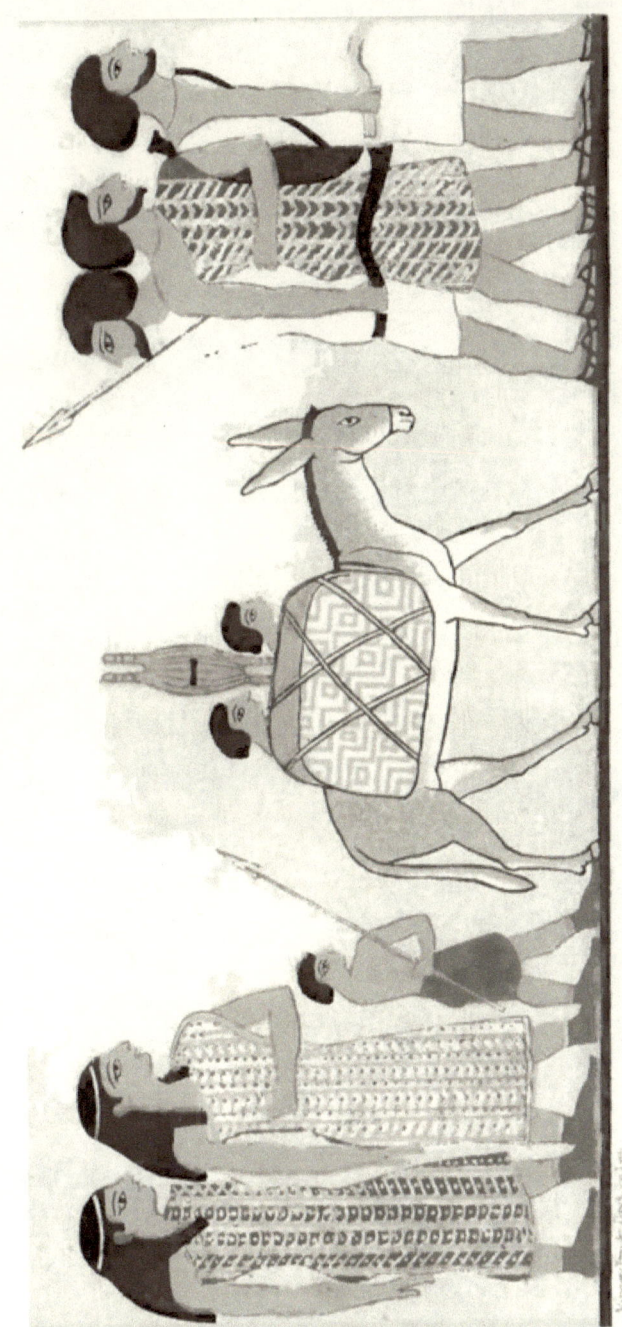

ASIATIC IMMIGRANTS.

one of the group is playing on a lyre of antique form. The children are carried in panniers, and women walk by their side; asses laden with baggage bring up the rear.

This occurred in the sixth year of Usertesen II., and it was a scene that was very likely oftentimes repeated. Families of foreigners came to settle in Egypt, attracted by its luxuriant plenty, and gradually developed into colonies. In the Delta more especially, foreigners settled in great numbers. There were colonists bent on peaceful industry, but there were others of a more restless and warlike type. It is possible that some may have been established there since the dark and troubled days that followed the sixth dynasty, when foreign tribes very probably held possession of part at least of the Delta for a time.

Egypt had often maintained a severe conflict on her southern frontier, where the boundary line was now marked by grim fortresses; but if trouble should ever overwhelm the land the storm would assuredly gather in the north-east. Fortresses had been erected there also, and Amenemhat's wall of defence was still standing, but there was no absolute line of demarcation. The north-east of Egypt was inhabited by many settlers, aliens, who were allied more or less closely in blood to restless and warlike peoples beyond the frontier.

Their presence was but of ill omen to the land of their adoption.

CHAPTER VII.

Invasion and Rule of the Hyksos—War of Liberation.
(*Circa* 2100-1600 B.C.)

The close of the twelfth dynasty was followed at no distant date by confusion and disaster. It appears, indeed, that the succeeding dynasty held for a time, at least nominally, the supremacy of Egypt; but sooner or later we find there was a rival dynasty (the fourteenth) ruling at Xois, in the Delta. To the kings composing it is assigned an average length of reign of little over two years, and this has led some to suppose that they were not in any sense Kings of Egypt, but were ruling in the Delta merely as governors—viceroys of foreign invaders. But all details, all records, fail us here, and we have no account of the events that led up to the crisis, when the long threatening storm broke over the land at last.

A warlike race, known to us as the *Hyksos*,[1] aided no doubt by the wandering tribes beyond the frontier, passed the north-east boundary of Egypt, seized upon the Delta, and set up their kingdom at Avaris, and were doubtless welcomed by the settlers of kindred blood already dwelling in the district. Egypt was weakened by discord; the dissensions of rival dynasties had probably led once more to the breaking up of the kingdom into small principalities; no united opposition could be offered to the invaders, and rival chieftains and kings were forced to acknowledge the supremacy of the stranger at the point of the sword.

The horse is never represented in Egyptian sculptures and drawings previous to this date, and if, as is most probable, the Hyksos invaders were mounted, it would be barely possible for foot soldiery to resist their progress. Memphis fell into their hands, and the Egyptian princes

---

[1] Probably *Hak-shasu*, or Princes of the Shasu. The Shasu were wandering tribes on the north-east, and it is not unlikely, Brugsch thinks, that this name was assigned them in derision of their claim to be considered Kings of Egypt. Kings of Egypt, indeed! No—haks (petty princes) of the Shasu they were. An accidental coincidence of meaning between Shasu and shepherd led to their being designated in later times 'Shepherd Kings.'

and governors as far south as Thebes were compelled to become their vassals and pay tribute. 'Under one of our kings,' says a native writer of later days,[1] in a fragment that has been preserved, 'it came to pass that God was angry with us, and men came from the East, who subdued our country by force, though we never ventured on a battle with them. When they had gotten our governors under their power, they burnt down our cities and demolished the temples of the gods. Their king lived at Memphis, and made the upper and the lower country pay tribute, and he left garrisons in fitting places. He strengthened Avaris greatly, building walls around it and filling it with armed men. These people and their descendants kept possession of Egypt for 511 years.'

The Egyptians might well have said, to use their favourite phrase, 'Never had the like been seen since the days of Ra.' There had been wars on the frontiers, and there had been one

[1] Manetho, the Egyptian priest, who, in the days of the Ptolemies, wrote a history of his country in Greek. It is, unfortunately, lost, excepting his list of kings and dynasties, and a few fragments quoted by later writers.

long dark period of division and civil war, but during the two or three thousand years that Egypt had been a kingdom no foreign foe had set foot upon her soil. Memphis, the 'secure and beautiful' city, had stood in all her splendour, and had never seen a hostile banner unfurled against her. The royal line of Mena had ruled,[1] the worship of the temples of Abydos and of the City of the Sun had prevailed uninterruptedly since the days of the pyramid builders and the 'old time before them.' It is a wonderful chapter in the world's history, and one turns the page with regret. Nor can we be surprised at the burning shame and bitter resentment with which the Egyptians of after times looked back upon those days of disgrace and subjection. As far as it was possible they obliterated every trace of the detested Hyksos supremacy; they chiselled out the names of their kings, and destroyed their monumental records. Very few traces survive, but it is plain, nevertheless, that the conquerors soon

---

[1] Even during the civil wars some branch of the ancient line was ruling, and it is probable that the eleventh dynasty was united by marriage to the early kings.

adopted Egyptian customs and Egyptian civilisation. The Hyksos kings assumed Egyptian titles and erected magnificent temples. And it is more than likely that the feelings of the native historians, galled and exasperated by the recollection of the harsh supremacy of aliens, considerably exaggerated the tale of the suffering and ruin entailed by their presence.

This period, of about 500 years' duration, is veiled from us in almost impenetrable darkness. The records left of themselves by the Hyksos Pharaohs were destroyed, and over the rest of the subject land there brooded the darkness of a long-protracted eclipse. The tribute was probably paid, and external quietude and order prevailed.

At length a ray of light dispels the darkness for an instant. 'It came to pass,' says an ancient papyrus, 'that the land of Khemi belonged to the enemy. No one was sovereign lord in the day when that happened. The King Sekenen-Ra ruled in the south, but the enemy ruled in the district of the Amu, and Apepi, their king, was in the city of Avaris; the whole land did him homage with the best of its handiwork. King Apepi took unto him Sutech for lord, refusing to serve any other god in the whole land, and he built for him a temple of enduring workmanship. King Apepi appointed festival days for making sacrifice to Sutech, as in the temple of Ra-harmakhu.' Here there is a break, after which the manuscript goes on to tell how King Apepi, by the advice of his learned councillors, sent an embassy to the ruler of the south (the tributary native prince, Sekenen-Ra). 'The ruler of the south said to the messenger, "Who sent thee hither? Why art thou come? Is it to spy out the land?"' So far as we can gather from the text (which is here again interrupted) the messenger's reply related merely to the construction of a certain well for cattle, although he adds that 'sleep had not come to him by day or by night until he had delivered his message.' 'The ruler of the south was amazed, and knew not how to reply to the messenger of King Apepi.' Here another vexatious break occurs in the story.

It is more than likely that a spirit of independence was awakening in the south, under the brave Sekenen-Ra, and even that certain secret preparations for an uprising might have been afoot; so that the Hyksos messenger may, after all, have been neither more nor less than a spy, although apparently charged with nothing but an innocent message concerning a tank. It is at any rate clear that Sekenen-Ra's heart misgave him. His answer indeed is missing, but we read that 'the messenger of King Apepi rose to depart to where his royal master was,' and that the Egyptian chief, who evidently felt that the die was cast, forthwith 'bade summon his mighty chiefs, his captains and expert guides.' He repeated to them the whole story of the 'words King Apepi had sent concerning them. But they were silent, all of them in great dismay, and wist not what to answer him, good or bad.' Here the papyrus breaks off suddenly, and darkness closes in again.

We are left to guess the sequel, but it seems as though we can see how the prince of the south cast off his allegiance and defied the Hyksos sovereign.

His successors bore the same name as himself, and also his family name of Taa. They were known as Taa the Great and Taa the Victorious, and followed up his bold initiative with vigour and success. It was very slowly, and only by hard fighting and step by step, that Egypt was won back from the stranger. But as these brave chieftains pushed their way northward, one tributary prince after another would take heart and join in the war of liberation. The horse must by this time have been naturalised and made use of throughout the land, and thus one terrible and fatal disadvantage would be removed. Old rivalries and minor jealousies would melt away under the influence of a common need and a common hope. Taa the Victorious prepared a flotilla of Nile vessels, two of which bore the significant names of the '*North*,' and the '*Going up into Memphis*.' Doubtless it was under him that the ancient capital was regained, after which all was ready for the final attack, in view of which he had made ready his little navy,—the attack which should drive the foe from his stronghold in the Delta, where by this time he was standing desperately at bay.

Taa the Victorious married his son Kames

to the Princess Aah-hotep, an heiress of the ancient line, and it was their son Aahmes who brought the great war of liberation to a triumphant close, and placed upon his brow the double crown of Upper and of Lower Egypt.

CHAPTER VIII.

The Eighteenth Dynasty—Queen Hatasu and Thothmes III.
(*Circa* 1600–1400 B.C.)

ON the east bank of the river, about 50 miles from Thebes, there stood in ancient times a strong fortified city, surrounded by massive walls of such thickness, that chariots might have been driven abreast upon them. Of the city itself nothing survives save ruins; but in the valley that lies eastward, behind the hills, are still to be seen long rows of tombs and memorial sanctuaries, where were laid to rest the heroes of the great war of liberation.

The whole district was ruled by native governors, tributaries of the Hyksos, throughout the whole period of the foreign supremacy, and the daily course of Egyptian life seems to have gone on with but little interruption. The tombs just mentioned belonged chiefly to one family, and the walls are adorned as usual with inscriptions and representations of scenes and events from daily life. Baba-Abana, head of the family, tells us that he was the parent of 52 children, and was able to provide abundant food and every necessary comfort for them all. 'If any one supposes I am jesting,' he adds, 'I invoke the god Munt to witness that I am speaking the truth.' Baba-Abana was an officer under Taa III. (the Victorious), and was no doubt actively engaged in helping forward the construction of the Egyptian flotilla. He tells us further of a famine that 'lasted for many years,' and that he provided corn for his city each year of the famine. This must have been the same famine that is mentioned in Genesis, when Joseph, at the court of the Hyksos Pharaoh, was providing corn for the land—the famine which led to the establishment of the Hebrew colony in the Goshen district of the Delta. Their presence there would be welcome, as they were no doubt of kindred race with those who then bore rule.

One of the numerous family of Baba-Abana, named Aahmes (like the king), did good service in the fleet during all the closing scenes of the war. He has left us an account of his doings, which opens thus:—'The Chief of the fleet, Aahmes, son of Abana (the Blessed), speaketh to you all, ye people, that you may know the honours that have fallen to his lot.' He was born, he tells us, in the city of Nek-heb (the Greek Eileithyia), and as a lad he served King Aahmes on board a ship called the '*Calf.*' He married, and set up a house, after which he was promoted, 'because of his strength,' to another vessel called the '*North.*' And when the king went out in his chariot, it was the duty of the young captain to follow him on foot. In the siege of the Hyksos stronghold, Avaris, he fought bravely on foot in presence of his majesty. During the siege he was further promoted to the vessel called '*Going up into Memphis.*'

Hard fighting went on around Avaris, and Aahmes tells us of the trophies of the dead [1] he brought in, as well as of his living prisoners. One of the latter he had much difficulty in securing, for he had to drag him some distance with a firm grasp through the water to avoid

---

[1] These were the hands of the slain, which were cut off and counted to ascertain the number of the fallen.

the road to the town. His prisoners were assigned to him as slaves, and many rewards and golden gifts were presented him for his services. Avaris was taken at length, and the Hyksos driven beyond the frontier, the king pursuing them as far as Sherohan, in Canaan, which town he also captured in the sixth year of his reign.

This was the final act of the long-protracted struggle in the north, but the mountaineers of Nubia were still in arms. There was sharp fighting in the south before the naval captain could record that his majesty 'had taken possession of the land, both of the north and of the south.' Aahmes received a gift of some acres of cultivated land in his native district. Later on we find him, as a veteran warrior, accompanying the two succeeding sovereigns on campaigns in the south, where he fought as admiral, at the head of the fleet. His final exploits were performed on a more distant field of battle—the 'land of the two rivers'— Naharina (Mesopotamia). There he captured a chariot, with its horses and charioteers, for which deed he received for the seventh time a

gift in gold. He concludes his story thus:—
'Now I have passed many days, and reached a grey old age. I too shall pass away to Amenti, and I shall rest in the tomb which I have prepared for myself.' And there may still be seen a portrait of the old sailor and of his wife. He is a 'bluff, resolute-looking man, not handsome; a short snub nose, and low solid brow—a short beard curling upwards from his chin.'[1]

The three monarchs under whom this distinguished officer served in succession, Aahmes, Amenhotep I., and Thothmes I., were the first three kings of the eighteenth dynasty. Aahmes inherited the throne by right of his mother's descent from Mena, but he strengthened his position further by himself marrying a princess of the royal line, Nefertari, who was greatly revered by succeeding generations, both as heiress in her own right, and as mother and ancestress of an illustrious dynasty.

The first twenty-two years of the reign of Aahmes were passed in unremitting warfare. After the capture of Sherohan, he followed his

---

[1] See *Nile Gleanings*, by Villiers Stuart.

foes no farther, but contented himself with erecting fortresses to protect the frontier. He would not feel his supremacy sufficiently assured over the numerous princes and chieftains who had gladly followed his victorious banner against the common foe, but would not have been quite ready when success had been achieved to resign their independent authority. At length, however, the king was able to lay aside his sword, and to turn his attention to the much needed work of restoring and renovating the temples of the gods. Again the limestone quarries were opened, and there are representations now to be seen in the sculptures of the huge blocks drawn along upon rollers by twelve or more oxen on the way to Memphis.

Aahmes left an infant son as heir to the crown, and the royal mother acted as regent until he was of age to reign. Amenhotep I. died young, and did not accomplish much; we learn, however, that during his reign Ta-Khent (Nubia) was mastered—' the land in its complete extent lay at the feet of the king.'

In the great discovery of coffins and royal mummies, made not far from Thebes in 1881, were brought to light the bodies of Taa the Victorious (the last of the brave Sekenen-Ras), of Aahmes, and of his son Amenhotep I. The conqueror of the Hyksos is enwreathed in garlands and festoons, his young son is swathed in lotus leaves and flowers—amongst them is a perfectly preserved wasp, that must have been accidentally shut in when the coffin-lid was closed more than 3000 years ago. This coffin and its case are in very good preservation; on the lid is an effigy of the young king, which is evidently a portrait. The coffin of Thothmes I. was found, but the mummy was missing.

When Thothmes I. became king, the internal dissensions of Egypt had quieted down, and, after one campaign in the south, the king proceeded to 'cool his heart' by undertaking the war on which the mind of the Egyptians was set—a war of retribution and of conquest. In this distant expedition (already alluded to in the memoirs of Aahmes), Thothmes rapidly pushed his way as far as Naharina (Mesopotamia), and returned home laden with treasures and spoil, having exacted a promise of annual tribute from many tribes in many regions. In the memorial chapel of the Thothmes family a sculpture is still remaining to tell of his triumphant home-coming. 'The soldiers holding branches in their hands, as emblems of peace, step out briskly as they approach their native land, and are met by a deputation of citizens, who slay fat oxen and sheep to feed them with. In the procession figure a couple of tigers, led along by their keepers,'[1] and apparently tame.

The king employed both his prisoners and his gold in continuing the construction of the great temple of Amen-Ra at Thebes. Its foundation had been laid by Amenemhat I. many centuries before, but the building had been hindered, or had altogether stopped, during the long years of foreign rule.

When Thothmes I. died, he left behind him one daughter and two sons, each of whom bore the same name as his father, but the younger of the brothers was only a little child. Their sister Hatasu was a proud ambitious woman, and had already been, to some extent, associated with her father during his reign. When

[1] *Nile Gleanings.*

Thothmes II. succeeded, she was formally associated with him in the government. We read but little about this king; his reign was brief, and he was probably outshone by the energetic partner of his throne. Hatasu, in fact, could ill brook even the slight restraint imposed by his co-regency, and no sooner was he dead than the proud queen, 'throwing aside her womanly veil, appeared in all the splendour of a Pharaoh—like a born king.'[1] She assumed man's attire, and was seen on state occasions in the dress and regalia of an Egyptian king— even to the plaited beard. She revered her father, and paid homage to his memory, but on the unfortunate Thothmes II. she hastened to avenge herself for the wrong he had done her in wearing a crown that was his own; she obliterated every trace of his existence to the best of her ability, and, vindictively erasing his name, she substituted her own. Hatasu also succeeded in having her name inscribed by the priests on the roll of Egyptian sovereigns.

Meantime the boy Thothmes, the rightful

---

[1] Brugsch, *History of Egypt*.

king, was sent by order of his imperious sister to the almost inaccessible marshes of the Delta, where he was doomed to wear out the years of his dreary boyhood, cherishing, there can be little doubt, the most vindictive feelings towards the sister who, having usurped his place, was ruling Egypt with splendour and renown.

No reign was more distinguished than that of Hatasu for art and architecture. She completed the magnificent temple begun during her joint reign with her brother. An avenue of sphinxes led up to the gate towers and the obelisks, which were 97 feet in height, and made of red granite capped with gold. The temple itself stood upon four broad and stately terraces, which rose one above another until they touched the dazzling marble-like limestone cliff against which they rested; the terraces were covered with hieroglyphic inscriptions and carvings in bas-relief. In the limestone rock above were excavated vast funeral chambers, and here were buried the queen's father and mother, a sister who died young, and Thothmes II. Here also Hatasu herself and Thothmes III. were laid in due time, but none of these royal mummies have been suffered to remain in peace. To avoid violation and plunder, it became customary some centuries later to examine and to report upon the state of royal tombs and coffins from time to time, and to remove them occasionally to securer resting-places. Thus it came to pass in the great discovery of 1881, the empty coffin of Thothmes I. was found, together with the coffin and mummy of his son and successor, Thothmes II.

To the architect Semnut, who so successfully carried out the grand conception of the terraced temple, his royal mistress raised a memorial—a statue in black granite in a sitting attitude of calm repose; on his shoulder is the inscription—'His ancestors were not found in writing,' *i.e.* they were unknown men, a not unfrequent phrase in Egyptian inscriptions. Semnut is represented as saying, 'I loved *him*, and gained the admiration of the *lord* of the country. *He* made me great, and I have become first of the first, clerk of the works above all clerks. I lived during the reign of

King Ma-Ka-Ra;[1] may *he* live for ever!' No doubt it was the general custom thus to flatter the foible of their sovereign, who was, in fact, designated by a name signifying 'Lady-King.'

Under the queen's rule, however, there was an entire cessation of military enterprises, for Hatasu did not so far assume the character of a Pharaoh as to put on armour and lead her troops to the battle-field. Egypt therefore enjoyed unbroken tranquillity during her peaceful and brilliant reign—a reign not only distinguished for the splendour of its architecture, but memorable also for an expedition to the land of Punt. This expedition is portrayed in curious and interesting detail upon the stages of the terraced temple. Long ago we know that the Egyptian imagination had been stirred by the supposed marvels of that 'sacred land' of dream and legend. And in the days of Hatasu the expedition sent thither by King Sankh-ka-ra, centuries before, would not have been forgotten. By the queen's command an embassy was despatched to its shores. Princes and lords were intrusted

---

[1] Honorific or crown name which Hatasu, like other Egyptian sovereigns, assumed at her accession, and which was distinct from the personal or family name.

with rich and royal gifts for the purpose of conciliating the people of that land over which the Lady-King desired to establish a supremacy, although not at the sword's point.

The expedition arrived in safety, and found the people inhabiting little dome-shaped dwellings, supported on piles and approached by ladders, under the shade of their cocoa-nut and incense trees. The Egyptians, with their strong turn for natural history, were much interested by the novelties they beheld around them, the unfamiliar plants and trees, the strange birds and animals not known in Egypt. All went well. Gifts were exchanged, and the natives promised to acknowledge the supremacy of Egypt, and to send an annual tribute thither. The king of the country appeared on the scene accompanied, say the hieroglyphs, 'by his enormously fat wife . . . an ass serves the fat wife to ride on.' This lady, the queen of the fairyland of Egyptian fancy, is in truth a painful object to behold; not merely fat but bloated, and swollen in such an extraordinary manner as to render it probable that, although the 'Queen of Punt,' she 'was a leper.'

Soon began the work of packing and of lading the transport vessels with the rare and beautiful products of the land. The busy scene is delineated upon the walls of the temple, and the inscriptions relate how the 'ships were laden to the uttermost with all the wonderful products of the land of Punt, with the precious woods of the divine land, with heaps of the resin of incense and fresh incense trees; with ebony and objects carved in ivory and inlaid with gold, with sweet woods and paint for the eyes, with dog-headed apes and long-tailed monkeys, with greyhounds and with leopards, besides some of the natives and their children.' The Egyptians, on the voyage home, were evidently much taken by the antics of the monkeys, as they sprang about amongst the sails, up and down the rigging. The fresh incense-trees, thirty-one in number, were carefully planted in tubs, and six men were assigned for the transport of each of them to the vessel which was to carry it north for transplantation into another soil.

Several of the princes and chief men of Punt accompanied the expedition on its return, and were received in state by the queen in her male attire. It is a pity we have no records that might convey the impression made by the wonders of Egypt upon the visitors in their turn. The rich treasures they had brought were offered by Hatasu to the god Amen-Ra with gladness and national rejoicings. The queen appeared in royal pomp; the priests carried in solemn procession 'the sacred bark' of the deity, before which the youthful Thothmes offered incense; the warriors of Hatasu's guard followed, bearing branches in their hands as signs of peace, and tumultuous cries of joy rent the air on all sides.

The appearance of Thothmes on the scene proves that the time had come when his claims could no longer be ignored nor he himself be detained amid the distant and dreary marshes of the Delta by the jealous fears of the queen. The sight of the brave and handsome youth who had been King of Egypt by right for fifteen years could hardly fail to win the people's hearts, and his imperious sister found herself at last compelled to let him take his place at her side, with what long suppressed feelings of rancour and ill-will may be readily imagined.

The coronation of Thothmes III. was celebrated with all fitting splendour and state, and, for a short time at any rate, the brother and sister ruled jointly. But Hatasu must have felt that her day was over, and after a little while her name silently disappears from the historic records. Of the close of her life we know nothing, but we know that Thothmes, with vindictive satisfaction, chiselled out her name wherever he could find it, and that he always dated the years of his own reign from the time of his brother's death, ignoring Hatasu's sovereignty as a usurpation.

The reign of Thothmes, thus reckoned, was a very long one, close upon 54 years, and much of it was passed by the warlike sovereign in other lands and upon distant battle-fields.

Nubia was by this time really an Egyptian province, and was governed by a viceroy, who was often one of the king's sons. In the gold-yielding districts a miserable population —prisoners, slaves, and criminals, were toiling beneath the scorching sun, extracting the gold from the stubborn stone; which had first to be hewn out, then crushed, and finally the grains of the precious metals to be washed out. Elsewhere the province was peopled by an active race, grouped around the temples, fortresses, and garrison towns, where they found employment, and received abundant supplies of food for their sustenance from Egypt; others were engaged in the navigation of the dangerous cataracts. The natives had grown accustomed to Egyptian rule, and were rapidly adopting Egyptian religion and civilisation. Their chief city Napata was indeed destined to become one day the seat of a strong Egyptian dynasty, and a stronghold of the worship of Amen-Ra.

There was therefore no cause for anxiety concerning the south, and the eyes of the young sovereign turned eagerly to the regions where his father had made his rapid campaign, and acquired military renown and abundant spoil. The policy of 'extending the frontiers of Egypt' was no doubt partly dictated by the desire of rendering the country safe from any further invasion, by subduing the neighbouring lands; but it is certain that the vision of establishing an Egyptian empire fascinated the imagination of Thothmes III., and he was able to realise the dream.

The course of Egyptian history had flowed on century after century, for 2000 or 3000 years, in a sort of majestic solitude, like its own mighty river, which for 1800 miles of its course receives no tributary stream. The people might be said to have 'dwelt alone.' The position of the land was isolated and secluded, its people had an innate dislike of the sea, and possessed no sea-going ships; they were perfectly content within the bounds of their own luxuriant domains, and knew and cared very little about the world that lay beyond. The frontiers were well guarded and no foe had crossed them, nor had any vision of conquest or wide-spread empire arisen to dazzle the imagination of the early kings.

The coming of the Hyksos had wrought a great change, and had broken down the barriers of isolation. And the mighty wave of national energy, which, gathering strength as it rose, swept away the foe, did not thus spend all its force. A longing arose for retribution, conquest, empire; the avenging campaign of Thothmes I. had stimulated rather than satisfied a national craving for glory and for wealth. The Pharaohs now emerge from the seclusion of the valley of the Nile, and enter that blood-stained arena—the battle-field of the nations—the Syrian and Mesopotamian lands. But the brilliant successes and far-reaching supremacy of the Egyptian arms ended at last in disaster and decline, from which there was no power of recovery.

Far enough, however, were any such gloomy forebodings from the thoughts of King Thothmes III., when he mounted his war chariot and assembled his troops upon the field of Zoan. The tributes promised to his father by the conquered princes had for a long time ceased to be paid. They knew that a female sovereign held the sceptre, and the tribes that had acknowledged the father's supremacy cast off all fealty to the daughter. The town of Gaza alone had remained faithful to the Egyptian allegiance. Here Thothmes took up his quarters for the night on the twenty-third anniversary of his accession (dating *i.e.* from his brother's death). Next morning he left the city, 'full of power and strength, to conquer the miserable enemy, and to extend the frontiers of Egypt, as his father Amen-Ra had promised him.'

The country known to us as Palestine or Syria was then, as at a later date, divided into several petty kingdoms, each with a fortified capital of its own. The general name by which its inhabitants were known to the Egyptians was that of the Rutennu, and at this moment their various tribes were allied against Egypt under the leadership of the King of Kadesh, and, encamped within and around Megiddo, they were waiting the attack of King Thothmes.

There was a choice of roads before the invading host. One broad highway led along the Mediterranean coast, keeping the sea in sight, until it turned in an easterly direction, and opened out finally upon the wide plain of Kadesh. Another way led along the banks of the Jordan, but it was a dangerous route, often very narrow and amongst thickets, where a foe might easily lurk unseen. After leaving the Jordan it went through the narrow valley of the Orontes until it also reached the capital of the King of Kadesh. Thothmes addressed his army, and told them of the information he had just received concerning the position of the enemy, who had said, 'I will withstand the King of Egypt at Megiddo.' 'And now,' said the king, 'tell me the way by which we shall go to break into the city.' The army with one accord entreated to be led by any way but that which wound along by the Jordan. 'It has been told us,' they said, 'that the foe lies there in ambush, and the way is impassable for a great host; one horse cannot stand there beside another, nor can one man find room by another. The army would be blocked, and be helpless before the enemy. There is a broad way that starts from Aluna, and it offers no opportunity for an attack. Whithersoever our victorious leader goes we will follow him, only we pray that he will not take us by the impassable way.' Thothmes decided on the broad road, and made the soldiers take an oath that they would not go on in advance of the king with any idea of protecting his person, but would let him take the place of danger at their head. Dismounting from his chariot, he advanced on foot in the forefront of the army. 'He went forward,' says the story; 'his divine father Amen-Ra was before him, and Horus-Hormakhu was at his side.'

In a few days the camp was pitched opposite Megiddo. 'Keep yourselves ready,' said the king, 'look to your arms, for we shall meet the enemy in battle early to-morrow morning.' And they set the watch, saying, 'Be of good courage; watch, watch—watch over the life in the king's tent.' Next morning the assault was made, but the Canaanites were unable to make a stand against the disciplined valour of the Egyptian troops; they fled at the first onset 'with terror on their faces.' The dead 'lay on the ground like fishes,' and the fugitives in their haste left behind them their horses and their chariots of gold and silver, and 'were drawn up by their clothes as by ropes into the fortress.' The king's own tent was captured on the field, amidst shouts of joy and of thanks to Amen-Ra. Megiddo itself was taken, and the victor entrenched himself there to await the submission and the tribute of the confederated princes. Then the chiefs of the land came to do homage to the king, and, though the civilisation of the Canaanitish tribes may not have been high, yet there was no lack, at any rate, of a certain splendour at their kings' courts. They were graciously received by the young conqueror, and laid rich gifts at his feet, gold, silver, and *lapis lazuli*—wheat, wine, and wool,—besides many suits of brazen armour and chariots plated with gold.

The capture of Megiddo opened the way to the more distant field of Mesopotamia. In former ages that country had been the seat of civilised and highly cultivated states,[1] but these kingdoms had fallen, probably before some foreign conquerors, about the time that the twelfth dynasty was ruling in Egypt. About the period of the Hyksos supremacy there seems to have been an empire established at Babylon which included Assyria as a province; but this again had passed away, and the country was broken up into a number of petty principalities, which it was no hard task for Thothmes to subdue and reduce to some sort of vassalage. Among the Asiatic princes who brought him tribute are named those of *Assur* and of *Babilu*.

---

[1] The literature and traditions of these early Chaldean states were preserved and highly prized by the Assyrians, who appear to have had none of their own.

The supremacy of the Egyptian crown may thus be said to have been acknowledged in some sort over the 'known world;' for the Egyptian horizon did not extend beyond the Mediterranean Sea, the Euphrates, and the range of Mount Taurus in Armenia. 'I have placed the boundaries of Egypt at the horizon,' said Thothmes III., 'and I have set Egypt at the head of all nations, because its people are united with me in the worship of Amen.'

These Asiatic campaigns were often renewed during this long reign; thirteen or fourteen such are recorded. Each was followed by a longer or shorter interval of peace. The principal episodes of the wars were sculptured in bas-relief upon the walls of the great temple at Karnak, where also was inscribed a careful geographical enumeration of the conquered peoples, and a record of the tributes they respectively paid. Full accounts were also preserved in the libraries attached to the temples; but the Egyptian archives have perished, and Egyptian history with them, except so far as it was carved on the enduring stone, or written in the few papyri that have survived the general wreck.

There is an inscription on the tomb of a valiant captain of Thothmes, named Amenemhib, in which he tells us of the campaigns he was engaged in by his master's side. 'I never left him,' he says; 'great was the valour of his arm.' Then he records his own deeds, and describes the rich rewards assigned him. Twice he saved the king's life when in imminent peril. 'I saw the lord of the two countries in the land of Ni; he was hunting 120 elephants for the sake of their tusks. The largest one of the herd rushed upon his majesty, but I cut his trunk, and escaped through the water between the rocks.' Another time the King of Kadesh had started a wild horse to run upon the king. 'I followed him as he dashed among the warriors, and I slew him with my sword, and cut off his tail, which I presented to the king as a trophy.' In the siege of Kadesh he led the party that stormed the walls. 'I broke them open; I led all the valiant. None other went before me.'

The return of the king and his army from these distant expeditions was a sort of triumphal procession. No presage or foreboding of future ill troubled the Egyptians as they looked out for the appearance of their hero king and welcomed him with rapturous acclamations. In his train came princes and princesses of Canaan, prisoners of war, and slaves. Slaves formed a portion of the tribute imposed upon the subject countries. Then came horses (amongst them snow-white and bay), wild goats and asses, zebras or humped buffaloes, together with wilder animals of rarer species—tigers, the cinnamon-coloured bear of Mount Taurus, and occasionally a young elephant. The wealth brought home by the conquerors was incalculable. From the fruitful land of Palestine, corn, oil olive, and honey; Phœnicia sent her merchandise gathered in from many lands— gold, silver, and gems; turquoise, ruby, and coral; copper and lead, besides cedar and other fragrant woods. Nor were there wanting specimens of skilled and splendid artistic workmanship. There were chariots richly adorned with silver and gold, costly stuffs and embroidery, and 'goodly Babylonish garments;' gold vases from North Palestine are especially mentioned, inlaid with precious stones; flowers were carved upon the rim, and the handles made in the shape of some animal. In addition there was the tribute that flowed in regularly from the South. The friendly inhabitants of Punt sent, in recognition of the Egyptian supremacy, gums and fragrant spices in abundance. Kush was now ruled by an Egyptian viceroy, who took care that the contributions should never fail—negro slaves, long-horned oxen, bloodhounds, apes, panther skins, ostrich eggs, ivory, ebony, and rare trees. The last-named item possessed a special interest for the Egyptians, who had a strong love for natural history. An artist has depicted some wonderful plants, cactuses and water-lilies from the southern lands, and underneath is the inscription :—

'Here are all sorts of plants and flowers from Ta-nuter. The king speaks thus, "I swear by Ra, I call Amen-Ra to witness that everything is plain truth. What the splendid soil brings forth I have portrayed, to offer it to my father Amen-Ra, in his great temple as a memorial for all time."' It is also recorded of Thothmes, at the close of one of his campaigns, that four new species of birds that were brought to him 'pleased the king more than all the rest.'

As might be expected, Thothmes did not neglect to immortalise his name by erecting or adorning the temples of the gods. His greatest work was the Hall of Columns, which he added to the great Temple of Amen, begun by Amenemhat I., and still incomplete. He appointed 'feasts of victory' to be celebrated on the festivals of Amen, thus linking his own name very closely with that of his god, and he enriched the temple with enormous donations, the mere enumeration of which would fill pages. Neither gold nor silver, cedar wood or precious stones, need be spared now when all that the world could offer of rich and rare was flowing in a constant stream to add to the 'treasures in Egypt.' Special mention is made, amongst countless other gifts, of a beautiful harp of silver and gold and precious stones, to sing the praises of Amen upon his splendid festival days. We read too of a great barge of cedar wood inlaid with gold[1] for the purpose of receiving the god when conducted in solemn procession down the

---

[1] This barge was presented in the reign of Thothmes IV.

river. Obelisks were also erected by Thothmes, which were 'reflected with their splendour on the surface of the sacred lakes like stars upon the bosom of Nut.' One of them is now standing forlornly on the Thames embankment.

Not only did Thothmes confer these numberless and costly gifts upon the temples, but he endowed them munificently. Gardens and arable lands were assigned them, and a fixed system of contributions for their support was established. He also appointed many of his foreign prisoners to the service of the temples and their gardens. Besides these, there were great numbers that he could employ upon the public works, whilst year by year the slaves who formed a part of the annual tributes came to add to the multitude of poor captives. The service was rigorous, and there can be little doubt that their lives were 'made bitter.' There is a representation still existing of a number of these bondmen engaged in brickmaking. Their faces are of the Asiatic type, and the following words are added by way of explanation :—' They work at the building with dexterous fingers; their overseers show themselves in sight. They obey the words of the great skilful lord who directs them. They are rewarded with wine, and all kinds of good things. They are building a sanctuary for the god. The overseer says thus to the labourers: "The stick is in my hand: be not idle."'

Severe oversight, tempered by free access to the 'flesh-pots of Egypt' was then, as at a later date, the portion of those to whom the land of Egypt was the 'house of bondage.'

There can be little doubt that the waste of life upon distant battle-fields, the employment of foreign slave labour, and the luxury born of immense accession of wealth, all combined to produce a demoralisation and a weakening of the Egyptian people in due course of time. For the present, however, all was joy and exultation. The king was never weary of extolling the gods who had shown him such distinguished favour, and their good-will and his devotion are depicted in every possible way. On one obelisk (the obelisk of the Lateran), we see, *e.g.* the king kneeling and offering wine to Amen-Ra seated on a throne, or adoring the

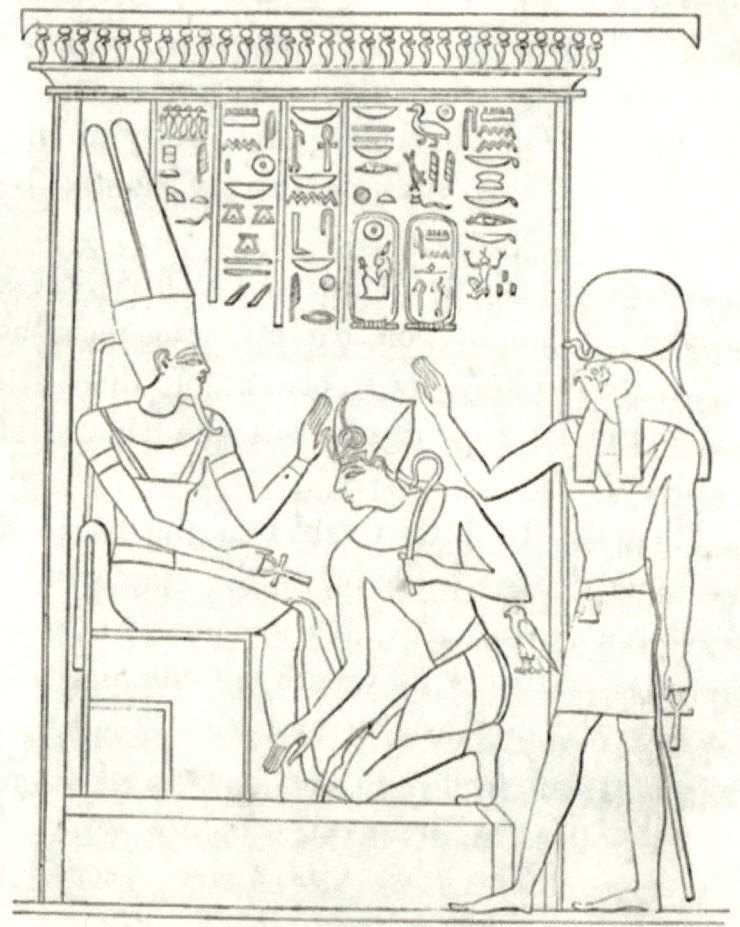

Amenhotep presented to Amen-Ra by Horus.

sacred hawk, symbol of Horus, to which he offers flowers, incense, and cakes of white bread. Again, Amen-Ra is seen taking him by the hand in token of his favour and protection, and at a memorial chapel in Nubia, the goddess Isis is represented as about to kiss the Egyptian monarch, whilst in another picture he is seen standing face to face with Sefek, the 'Lady of Writings.'[1] It is evident, therefore, that it had become customary and familiar to represent the deities, who are but seldom delineated in the pictures and sculptures belonging to the earlier dynasties. They are depicted in various ways. Sometimes it is in human form with some symbol or emblem attached or held in the hand, but very often the head of the deity is represented by that of the animal which, for some reason or other, was his symbol. Thus Horus is seen with a hawk's head, Thoth with that of an ibis. Isis is delineated not only as a woman, but as a cow, and sometimes as a woman with a cow's head. The Egyptians never appear to have even attempted to embody the divine majesty or beauty in any statue or picture. But certain objects, animate and inanimate, were regarded as symbolic, and as

[1] These two pictures are given in *Nile Gleanings*.

such were attached to the figures of the gods.[1] Of course they were not intended to be in any sense works of art, which such strange unnatural objects could never be; nor were they regarded as actually representative of the deities, which would have been simply absurd and profane, but they were emblematic signs of the divine attributes and nature, and were understood and recognised as such.

In one tablet at Karnak, Thothmes III. is depicted offering wine and incense to his father Amen-Ra, and the accompanying inscription is an heroic poem or hymn which must have been composed towards the close of his victorious reign. In it the god himself recounts all that he has brought to pass on behalf of his 'son.'

'Come to me,' he says, 'and rejoice in beholding my favour towards thee, O my son Men-kheper-Ra,[2] thou who livest for evermore! I am glorified by the vows thou renderest; my heart is glad when thou draw-

[1] It is comparatively easy to understand the choice of certain animals as symbolic (see on p. 198), but it is impossible to comprehend how an ostrich feather came to be the emblem of Ma, goddess of truth, or a shuttle the sign of Neith, goddess of wisdom. A certain resemblance in name seems sometimes to have suggested the symbol.

[2] Honorific or crown name of Thothmes III.

est near to my temple; dear unto me is the piety that has set up mine image within my sanctuary.

'Lo! I do reward thee—in that I give thee power and victory over all nations, for it is through me that the fear of thee resteth upon the whole earth and extendeth unto the pillars of heaven.

'I stretch forth my hand—for thee do I gather together the Annu by tens of thousands, and the northern people in myriads. By me have thine enemies been overthrown under thy feet. Thou hast penetrated into every land, but none has dared to set foot within thy borders, though I have protected thy steps when thou wast within their boundaries. Thou hast passed over the broad rivers of Mesopotamia; thy war-cry has re-echoed within the caverns of their hiding-places. I have bereft their nostrils of the breath of life.

'I am come and I have given thee to smite the princes of Tahi (Syria); I have made them behold thee like the star that flameth and that sendeth down the evening dew.

'I am come, and I have given thee to smite

the Western lands; I have made them behold thee like a young bull valiant in his might—he hath sharpened his horns—none may resist him.

'I am come, and I have given thee to smite all lands; I have made them behold thee as it were a crocodile: terrible is he exceedingly, and lord of the waters—none dare approach him.

'I am come, and I have given thee to smite the Tahennu in their islands; I have made them behold thee as a lion in his wrath—he lieth down upon the bodies of his prey and taketh his rest in the valleys.

'I am come, and I have given thee to smite the dwellers by the water-side that they who abide by the great sea may be subdued beneath thy feet; I have made them behold thee even like the king of birds who marketh his prey from on high, and seizeth upon whatsoever he listeth.

'I am come, and I have given thee to smite the dwellers in the waste; the Herusha are led captive; I have made them behold thee as it were the jackal of the South—he hunteth

AMENHOTEP ON THE LAP OF A GODDESS.

throughout the land, and he hideth his path in the darkness.

'I am he that hath watched over thee—oh my son beloved! Horus crowned in Thebes!'

Thothmes III. reigned very nearly 54 years. His faithful attendant Amenemhib, whose prowess had saved his master from the elephant and the wild horse, lived long enough to record that master's end.

'So after many years of victory and power,' he says, 'the King ended his course. He took his flight upwards into heaven and was joined unto the company of Ra. When the morning broke and the sky grew bright then was King Amenhotep (may he live for ever!) seated upon his father's throne; crowned like Horus, son of Isis, he took possession of Khemi.'

The magnificent terraced temple of Hatasu formed the mausoleum of the Thothmes family; but, like his predecessors, Thothmes the Great has not been suffered to remain undisquieted in the tomb. It was not far off from Hatasu's temple that his mummy also was discovered. The coffin was much injured, and the mummy itself broken into three pieces—the mutilated remains of this mighty Pharaoh are lying in the Museum at Boulak.

After the death of their conqueror, the kings of Canaan and the princes of Mesopotamia threw off the foreign yoke. Amenhotep II. overran the country and reduced its inhabitants once more to subjection. It is recorded of him that he smote down and slew seven of the Canaanitish chiefs with his battle-axe, and brought them back with him to Egypt. 'Six of these enemies,' says the story, 'were hung upon the walls of Thebes, and their hands were hung up in the same way; the other enemy was brought up the river to Nubia, and hung upon the walls of the town of Napata ' to show to the people of the land of the negroes for all time the victories of the king over his enemies.' This is the chief event recorded of the reign of Amenhotep II., who was succeeded by Thothmes IV.

CHAPTER IX.

The Eighteenth Dynasty—*continued.* (*Circa* 1600-1400 B.C.)

OF the reign of Thothmes IV. there is very little record left excepting the curious story of his own youth, which was written on a tablet suspended by his order upon the breast of the Sphinx at Ghizeh—to the following effect:—
'Thothmes had been practising spear-throwing in the neighbourhood of Memphis, where he also slung brazen bolts at a target and hunted lions in the "valley of the gazelles."[1] The prince rode in his two-horsed chariot, and his horses were swifter than the wind. With him were two of his servants. No man knew them. The hour came when he gave his servants rest. Thothmes went alone to the little sanctuary between the outstretched paws of the great

[1] This valley lay west of the pyramids in the Libyan desert, and was a favourite resort of sportsmen for hunting lions and other wild animals.

image of Horus in the city of the dead, to present an offering of the seeds of flowers upon the heights, and to pray to the "great mother Isis" and to other deities. A great enchantment rested on this place since the beginning of time even as far as the district of Babylon,[1] the sacred road of the gods to the western horizon. To the spot where the prince was standing the inhabitants of Memphis and the surrounding country were wont to come, to raise their hands in prayer and offer oblations. It so chanced that on one of these feast days the prince arrived at this spot about the hour of mid-day, and he laid himself down to rest in the shade of this great god until sleep overtook him. The sun was in the zenith when he dreamed, and lo! this great god spoke to him with his own mouth as a father speaks to his son. "Behold me, look at me, my son Thothmes! I am thy father Hormakhu-Ra. The kingdom shall be given thee; thou shalt wear the white crown and the red crown on the throne of the earth god Seb. The world shall be thine in its length and its breadth;

---

[1] This district of 'Babylon' was that where Cairo now stands.

plenty and riches shall be thine, the best from the interior of the land, and rich tributes from all nations. Long years shall be granted thee: my heart clings to thee.

'" The sand of this region in which I dwell has covered me up. Promise me that thou wilt do that which my heart desireth; then shall I know whether thou indeed art my helper." The prince awoke and repeated these words, and understood their meaning; and he laid them up in his heart, saying to himself—" I see how the people of this city honour the god with sacrificial gifts without ever thinking of freeing from sand the noble image of Hormakhu."'

The tablet here breaks off, but no doubt it recorded the fulfilment by Thothmes of the god's request.

Amenhotep III., successor of Thothmes IV., maintained with vigour the supremacy of Egypt both in the north and in the south. He must have been no ordinary sportsman if he speared, as he is said to have done, 102 lions with his own hand in the forest lands of Mesopotamia. His conquests were principally achieved in the south; for the sake of gold quite as much as for increase of territory he carried his arms into the Soudan, and subdued the negro peoples who dwelt beneath its burning sun. But the chief glory of Amenhotep III. was not won by spearing lions in Asia or conquering negroes in Africa; his name is remembered chiefly through his architectural achievements at Thebes. He erected a splendid gate-tower before the great temple at Karnak, and planned the avenue of sphinxes which connected it with another temple which he began at Luxor. To the north and south of the great temple he also built two smaller ones. On the western bank he constructed another and a magnificent temple.

His architect and namesake, Amenhotep, has left some notices of his own life and labours. 'The king appointed me under secretary. I studied the holy book and beheld the glories of the god Thoth. I was acquainted with the sacred mysteries, and was a master in the art of speech.' Amenhotep was besides intrusted with the charge of the royal household and the collection of the revenue, and he was commander-in-chief of the king's forces. All his varied services, however, might have sunk into obli-

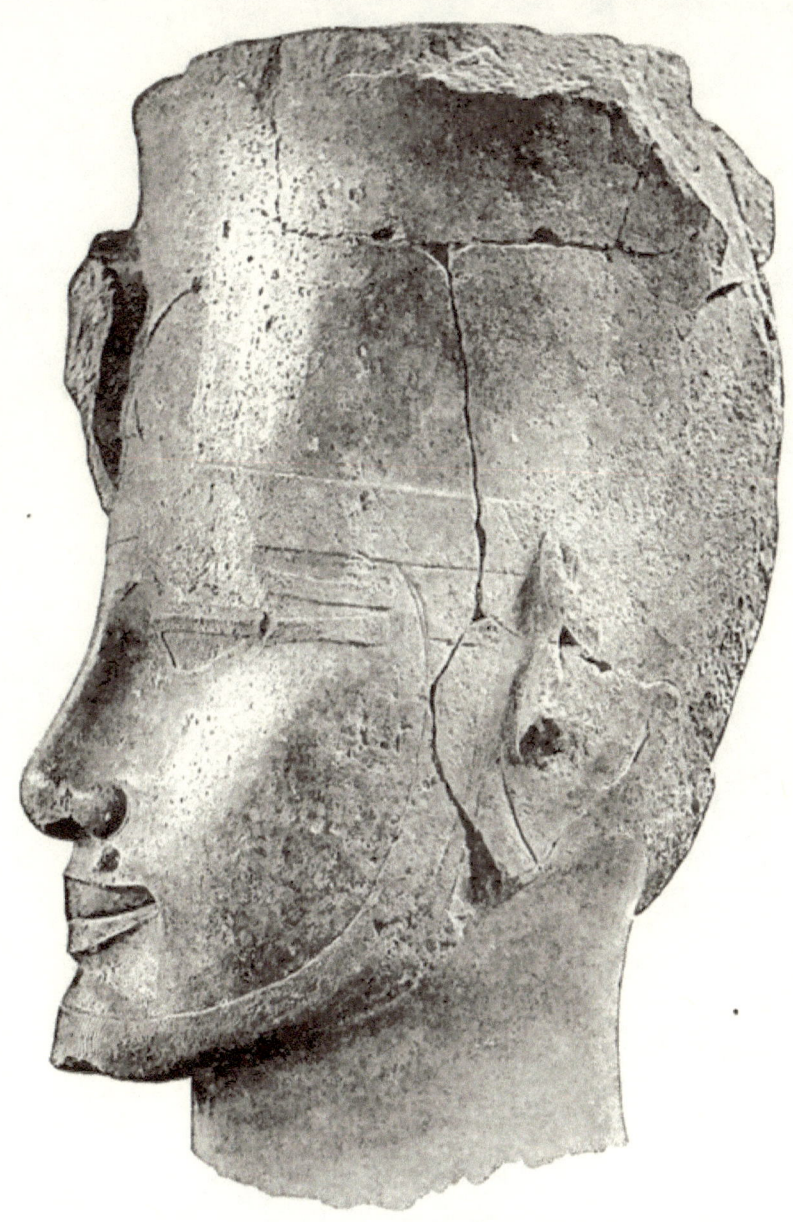

AMENHOTEP III. FROM A SCULPTURE IN THE BRITISH MUSEUM.

vion for later ages had it not been that in his capacity of chief architect he devised a scheme for immortalising the memory of his royal

The Colossi at Thebes.

master by the execution of two portrait statues 'in noble hard stone for his great building,' in

Western Thebes. These colossal statues were about 60 feet high, and each was cut out of a single block of stone. Amenhotep caused eight ships to be built to convey them down the river; he tells us that all the masons under his direction were full of ardour in the work, and that the safe arrival and landing of the statues at Thebes was a 'joyful event.' 'Every heart,' he says, 'was filled with joy, and the people shouted in praise of the king.' They were raised in their appointed place some little distance in front of the new temple the king had founded on the western side of the river. And he tells us that 'they made the gate-towers look small. They were wonderful for size and height, and they will last as long as heaven.'

A few scattered ruins only of the temple remain, but these two battered giants sit there still and keep their watch upon the desert plain. These were the statues called by Greek fancy the 'statues of Memnon,' who was, they said, the son of Aurora, and came to the aid of the Greeks at the siege of Troy. One of them was broken in two during a terrible earthquake that wrought great destruction in Egypt in A.D. 27.

The upper part fell to the ground, and it was after this event that the statue became vocal, and emitted every morning at sunrise a musical and melancholy strain. The fact of such a sound being heard was attested by an immense number of inscriptions left there by both Greek and Roman travellers. Septimius Severus afterwards repaired the statue, and from that time the phenomenon ceased, but has ever since been subject of curious speculation.

As might be supposed from the extent and splendour of his works, the reign of Amenhotep III. was not of short duration. We read of one thirty years' jubilee that was celebrated amid national rejoicings. Some of the taxpayers brought, it is said, on that occasion 'when the overseer had spoken but one word, more than the actual amount due, and the king rewarded their devotion by the presentation of golden chains and collars — the customary badges of honour.'

The portraits of Egyptian kings and queens bear every sign of being truthful and characteristic likenesses. The kings of the Thothmes family are all fine-looking men, their noses straight, their features well formed; those of the second and third Thothmes being particularly refined and delicately cut. And Queen Tai-ti, wife of Amenhotep III., is unquestionably the most beautiful amongst the Egyptian queens that we know. But the monarch who reigned next, or next but one to the last-named sovereign, is of quite peculiar ugliness; he has a retreating forehead, a very long aquiline nose, and an extraordinary chin, long and pointed. His figure is thin and effeminate, his legs feeble and attenuated, and his expression somewhat idiotic. It is difficult to believe that he could have belonged to the same family, or even the same nation as the Thothmes and Amenhoteps, his predecessors, and one is inclined to conclude with Mr. Villiers Stuart,[1] that a princess must have unexpectedly succeeded to the throne whose husband was a foreigner. This idea would agree with the fact that the new sovereign actually introduced a new form of worship into the country.

The mysterious god of Thebes was wor-

[1] See the *Nile Gleanings*, where the portraits of the sovereigns are given. If Khu-en-aten's is a caricature even, it is a caricature founded on a different type of countenance.

shipped under the name and figure of the sun, but this was regarded as only one of his manifestations, who was a being 'of many names, of holy transformations, of mysterious forms.'[1] But the new king worshipped Aten or the sun's disk, and recognised no other god. He also adopted the name of Khu-en-aten or 'Splendour of the Disk.' It is hard to understand theological controversies of so very ancient a date, but it is easy to feel what must have been the indignation among the priests and people at Thebes, when a royal edict was issued commanding that the names of Amen and of Mut should be erased from all the monuments in this, the ancient seat of their worship. Royal authority, however, proved sufficient to accomplish this outrage upon the national faith, but the king's further scheme of erecting a temple to his god Aten in Thebes itself could not be carried out, the influence of the rich and powerful priesthood and the strength of the national feeling were too great.

Khu-en-aten therefore abandoned Thebes altogether, and migrated with his court to a

[1] From a chapter in the Ritual.

spot about midway between that city and Memphis. Here he built an entirely new city and a splendid temple, with fire altars in honour of Aten. He summoned the masons of all Egypt to his work, and called together the chief men of the people, most of whom must have rendered but a sullen and unwilling obedience. There were courtiers, however, ready to adopt the royal creed, and to become, some of them at least, its zealous advocates. Amongstthese the foremost was one Meri-ra, who was promoted to the dignity of chief seer. 'Be thou chief seer of the disk of the sun according to thy wish,' said the king, 'for thou wast my servant who wast obedient to the teaching. Thou treasurer of the chamber of silver and gold! reward the chief seer of Aten —place a gold chain around his neck, and join it behind—place gold at his feet, because he was obedient unto the teaching of the king.'

At Tel-el-Amarna, east of the Nile, are still to be seen the ruins of this great and hastily constructed city, which was about two miles in length, but very narrow in width. Travellers say that the ground-plan of the houses may still be traced, and that there are some immense mounds covered by the drifting sand, where temples and palaces might be buried. Four miles off are tombs and rock temples excavated in the hill-side, but often entirely blocked up by sand. Wherever the new worship was portrayed, the sun's disk is represented above, with long rays reaching downwards, and each ending in a hand—the sign of divine protection; the hand often holds the symbol of life before the king.

The family life of Khu-en-aten is depicted more than once. In one group he is seen with his queen Nefer-tai and their young daughters, distributing gifts of honour at some festival. One little boy is there too, but he is too young to take part in the distribution, and is caressing his mother's face. Strong affection appears to have united the royal family, who doubtless felt their position a very isolated one. The prayers and praises, however, that are recorded as forming part of the new ritual, are very similar in tone and expression to those used in the customary worship. Prayer for the reigning sovereigns is frequent; on one festive occasion we read that the king gave his city the name of 'Delight of the Sun's disk,' and offered sacrifices with solemn invocation. 'Tender love fills my heart for the queen and her young children. Grant long years of life to Nefer-tai, that she may keep the king's hand. Grant long life to the royal daughters, that they may keep the hand of the queen, their mother, for evermore.' Nefer-tai appears to have died comparatively young; in one of the sculptures she is represented 'with terrible fidelity,' Mr. Villiers Stuart says, as apparently in the last stage of wasting disease. Her only son must have died quite in childhood; he is not represented again, but the daughters, seven in number, are frequently seen. As Khu-en-aten died without a male heir, the crown passed to his daughters' husbands, two if not three of whom reigned in succession. They soon returned to Thebes, and to the worship of Amen-Ra, but none of them were ever acknowledged as true-born kings; it is doubtful whether they were crowned at Thebes. Ai was the last of them, and a beautiful rose-coloured sarcophagus of granite found in a tomb to the west of the

SUCCESSORS OF KHU-EN-ATEN. 137

royal sepulchres bears his cartouche.¹ It is worthy of notice that he is styled *prince*, not king. Each of these rulers, in fact, occupied the throne only in right of his wife,² and were themselves apparently merely officers in high position at Khu-en-aten's court—a fact sufficient to account for the coldness with which the priests of Amen regarded them, in spite of their official return to the national worship. The government, however, appears to have been well administered by them, and foreign tributes were duly paid. A scene is represented on the walls of a tomb at Thebes, in which the governor of the south (whose tomb it was) is introducing a negro queen into the presence of Tutankh-amen, one of these princes. She has come in person to lay tribute and gifts at his feet. The boats are depicted in which the party have travelled and brought with them giraffes and leopards from the South, which are now presented to the king with other offerings, amongst which is a model of one of the negro dome-shaped huts with palm trees,

---

¹ The oval in which the royal names are always inscribed.

² And the wives, *in all probability*, inherited only through their mother, Khu-en-aten's wife.

around the tops of which giraffes are nibbling. The dark-hued princess made use of a sort of chariot drawn by oxen; her offerings are by no means devoid of artistic merit, though they cannot vie, in this respect, with those presented at the same levée by Asiatic princes of red complexion, and long curling black hair; they bring costly works wrought in gold, silver, and precious stones—the produce of skilled Phœnician art.

None of these kings apparently left any children. The official lists of sovereigns do not include any names between that of Amenhotep III. and Horus. It was to Horus that all eyes turned when the direct succession failed. He was then living in retirement at a city called Ha-Suten in middle Egypt, but had held high office at court at one time, and had been promoted to the dignity of 'guardian,' and afterwards of 'Adon' or 'Lord,' of the land—if indeed he had not been in some way recognised as heir to the throne itself. Horus was esteemed and beloved for the uprightness and gentleness of his character. 'He took pleasure in justice,' it is said of him, 'which he

carried in his heart; he followed the gods
Thoth and Ptah in all their ways, and they
were his shield and protectors on earth for
evermore.' He was especially acceptable to
the priesthood on account of his fervent attach-
ment to the old faith and the national gods
—the god Horus being regarded as his special
patron and guardian. To him was ascribed
his elevation to the royal dignity. 'Horus
made his son great, and willed to prolong his
life until the day came when he should receive
the office destined for him.' It is doubtful
whether he was himself of royal descent, but it
is certain that he married a princess of the
direct line, and that no one else was thought of
for a moment when the throne became vacant.
There is a long account preserved of his
accession, and solemn reception, and coronation
at Thebes. 'Heaven and earth rejoice together
—the gods invested him with the double
crown. Heaven kept festival, and all the land
was glad. The deities rejoiced on high, and
the people of Egypt raised their rapturous
songs of praise even unto heaven; great and
small united their voices with one accord. It

was as if Horus, son of Isis, were once more presenting himself after his triumph over Set.'

The new king was indeed regarded as, in some sense, an avenger triumphing over evil. One can imagine that even though the previous rulers had returned to Thebes and its gods, it would have been hardly possible for their wives, who must have shared their sovereignty, to indulge in any bitter animosity towards the city in which they had been brought up, towards the worship which their father had established there, or towards the names and memory of their parents. But at the accession of Horus, all restraint was removed, and the full tide of animosity let loose against the 'city of the delight of the sun's disk.' City, temples, and tombs were destroyed, and every vestige and trace of the reign and the religion of Khu-en-aten effaced as far as possible. The stone was taken to be employed in the building of Theban temples. Only a few ruins and a few inscriptions have escaped to tell the traveller of this curious episode in Egyptian history.

Equal diligence was shown by this sovereign in rebuilding and beautifying the temples which had long been neglected. The cities of the gods, we are told in decidedly hyperbolical language, 'lay as heaps of rubbish.' 'He renewed the temples of the sun-god,' we read, 'and Ra rejoiced to see that renewed which had been destroyed in former times.' The king also provided for the sacrifices; he appointed holy persons, singers, and body-guards for the temples, and assigned for their use and service arable land, cattle, and all that was required—that 'they might sing thus each new morning unto Ra: "Thou hast made the kingdom great for us in thy son the delight of thy heart, King Horus. Grant him length of years and victory in all lands, even as unto Horus, son of Isis."'

Horus reigned for more than twenty years, and his death was followed by the accession of a new dynasty—the nineteenth.

CHAPTER X.

The Nineteenth Dynasty (*circa* 1400-1200 B.C.) Rameses the Great.

THE peace of Egypt was not disturbed, although the direct succession again failed at the death of Horus. It is more than doubtful whether the soldier Rameses who now came to the front was of the royal line at all. He married his son Seti to a princess of the house of Pharaoh, and associated him with himself in the government. After a brief reign, of which next to nothing is recorded, he died, and left the crown to Seti. The wife of this sovereign was regarded with reverence as the descendant of the ancient line; and her claim to remembrance in after times was not so much that she was the wife of Seti, as that she was mother of Rameses II., in whose person the direct line was again restored. The child was associated with his father from a very early age, so that at any rate the sanction of a true-born Pharaoh might be given, however nominally, to all that was done.

The reign of Seti I. was not long, but it was full of stirring events, which are recorded on a wall of the great temple at Karnak. Egypt had been absorbed in religious and domestic dissensions, and her claims to supremacy and empire in Asia had been allowed to lapse. Encouraged by this apparent indifference, the wandering Shasu tribes had ventured to cross the frontier, and had entered the Delta. Seti was a man of war, and was no doubt glad at heart to veil the obscurity of his birth and his doubtful right to the crown in a dazzling cloud of military triumph and renown. He marched against the intruding Shasu, and soon discomfited them. 'The king was against them as a fierce lion; not one escaped to tell of his strength to the distant nations,' it is said. Nevertheless, we find them soon after able to rally and make a stand upon Phœnician soil with the Phœnicians as allies. The king, whose horses on this occasion bore the name, 'Amen gives him strength,' again attacked and overthrew them; then, turning upon their allies, he defeated them also, the Egyptian chariots meeting the Phœnician in furious encounter. Afterwards he marched upon the Rutennu (Canaanites), and his horses were called 'big with victory.' So rapid was his success, that his approach took the great Syrian stronghold of Kadesh unawares. Herds and flocks were quietly pasturing under its walls when the Egyptian army appeared in sight. In hot haste herds and herdsmen fled within the city walls for shelter; the garrison forthwith made a sally, but Seti was too strong for them, and the fortress was stormed and captured.

A more formidable enemy remained. Northwards from Syria dwelt the powerful nation of the Kheta (or Hittites), who now appear upon the scene for the first time. Over their well-ordered hosts likewise Seti claims a victory. 'As a jackal,' say the inscriptions, 'he rushes through the land and seeks after his prey—he is as a fierce lion that haunteth the most hidden paths in every land—as a mighty bull that hath whetted his horns for the strife. He hath smitten down the Asiatics, and thrown the

Kheta to the ground; their princes hath he slain by the sword.' It is quite plain, nevertheless, that the Egyptian monarch was glad enough to conclude a peace on equal terms with his brave opponents, and to return home again. On his way he visited the country of Limmanon (Lebanon) to procure cedar trees for the construction of a vessel to be used in the processions of Amen-Ra, and for the erection of the masts on the gate-towers of the temple. The people of that region received him with every mark of friendliness and respect; they are seen in the pictured story busily engaged in cutting down the tallest and finest of the trees for the service of the king.

Seti re-entered Egypt in triumph, laden with rich spoil; he was greeted with acclamations, and welcomed with peaceful offerings of fragrant flowers, songs of victory, and shouts of exultation. 'Thou hast triumphed over thy foes, and hast quenched the fury of thy heart. Ra himself has established thy boundaries. His hand has protected thee when thy battle-axe was raised aloft above the heads of thine enemies; their kings fell by thy sword.'

No doubt in this blaze of glory and glitter of spoil all remaining misgivings as to the 'right divine' were dispelled and forgotten, especially as in a succeeding campaign the boy Rameses accompanied him. From his very birth this boy had been the object of regard and almost of devotion. He is seen in early infancy caressed by his mother and the ladies of the court. Later on he stands by his father's side doing homage to his ancestors or to the gods in the temple of Abydos. On state occasions he occupied a prominent position, and was the central point of interest—the idol of his parents, and the hope of the nation, who cherished a real and most effective belief in the divine right of the god-descended race of their sovereigns. In a small Nubian temple is a sculpture, in which the youth is represented as returning from his first campaign, and receiving a loving welcome from his mother. She has noble features, as became her lineage, and there is a likeness between her and her son—so that although she is represented as a goddess, the face is no doubt intended as a portrait. The campaign from which she welcomes home her son, was against the Libyans, and, not unlikely, he stood by his father's side when the chariot, drawn by horses called 'Victorious is Amen,' fell upon the foe. 'He utterly destroyed them,' it is said, 'as they stood upon the field of battle; they could not hold their bows, and they remained hidden in their caves like foxes, for fear of the king.'

Seti again celebrated a triumph, and dedicated his spoil to Amen-Ra, together with the prisoners, whom he gave to the service of the temple, both as men and women servants. 'The kings of the nations that did not know Egypt,' so they sang on the occasion, 'are brought by Pharaoh. They magnify his mighty deeds, saying: "Hail to thee, King of Egypt! Mighty is thy name. Happy is the people that is subject to thy will, but he who oversteppeth thy boundaries shall appear led in chains as a prisoner. We did not know Egypt; our fathers had not entered it. Grant us freedom out of thy hand."'

The events of Seti's campaigns are sculptured on the north wall of his Hall of Columns at Karnak. He is spoken of there as taking an intense and ferocious delight in battle. 'Dear to him is the fray! his delight is to dash therein; his heart is satisfied when he beholds streams of blood gush forth, and strikes off the heads of his enemies. One moment of the strife of men is more precious to him than a whole day of pleasure. With one stroke he smiteth down the foe and spareth none, and whosoever is left alive he carrieth down into Egypt alive as a prisoner.' So keen and savage a delight in bloodshed has confirmed some writers in the idea that Seti came of some alien race, as it is out of harmony with the mildness and humanity that characterised the Egyptian character. His name is considered as probably showing a close connection with the Delta, where Set was worshipped, chiefly by the foreign settlers; whilst the name of that god was so hateful in Egyptian eyes that it was chiselled away from the monuments, both during Seti's life and after his death, even though it occurred as part of the royal name, and the king himself appears frequently to have changed his own objectionable name for that of Osiris. It may also be noted that the type of face of the sovereigns of the nineteenth dynasty is different from that of the preceding kings, and is decidedly of a more Semitic cast.

Although Seti had reconquered Syria, and possibly the adjacent lands, it does not seem that the stream of tribute flowed in such abundance as during the reign of Thothmes the Great. Treasure, however, was required, and the king resolved to have the valley of Hammamat thoroughly explored and worked. He went there himself in the ninth year of his reign, for, as the inscription says, 'his heart wished to see the mines whence the gold is brought.' Water was, of course, the first necessity as of old in the days of the eleventh dynasty, and Seti visited the hills in company with those who knew most about the watercourses. The desolation of the hot waterless valleys struck the king. After a journey of some miles he is said to have halted to meditate quietly, and he 'said within himself, "If the road be without water the wayfarers must perish; they die of parching thirst. Where shall I find a place where the burning thirst may be quenched? Vast is this region, and far does it extend. He who is here overtaken by thirst will cry out, 'O this land of perdition!' Those who come hither will come to perform their obligations towards me; I must do that which will enable them to live. Thus shall my name be venerated throughout future generations."' When the king had said thus within himself he went up into the hills to found there a sanctuary wherein prayer might be offered to the god. After that it pleased him to assemble workmen to quarry the stone, and to form a reservoir there amongst the hills for the purpose of sustaining the fainting by giving him fresh water in the time of the summer heat. And the water came in great abundance, like the waters of the Nile at Abu. The king spake and said, 'The god has heard my prayer; the water has come forth abundantly out of the rocks; the road that had no water has been made good under my reign. The shepherds shall have pasture for their flocks.'

A town was afterwards built at this new centre of industry, and a temple erected where Seti offered worship 'to his fathers the gods.' Guards were appointed to protect the convoyers of the precious metal, which was largely used by the king in adorning both temples and statues of the gods. Indeed, all the works ascribed to this reign are remarkable for their beauty and perfect finish, so that Seti I. can hardly be looked upon, after all, as nothing more than a man of blood and a lover of the fray. The chief of his works is a grand Hall of Columns that he added to the Great Temple at Karnak, founded so long before by Amenemhat I. It contained 134 immense columns of massive proportions, but, like his other undertakings, it had to be left incomplete, as his reign was not of long duration. In one of the corridors of his beautiful temple at Abydos was found the famous 'Tablet,' so invaluable to students of Egyptian history. It contained the names of 76 royal ancestors of Rameses II., going back to King Mena himself; and the young Rameses is seen standing by his father and offering homage to their memories; on the opposite wall are inscribed the names of the Egyptian gods and goddesses, and a beautifully executed bas-relief represents the prince, under his father's direction, pouring out in honour of the deities a libation, which is received into a vessel full of flowers.

The strong affection borne by Seti to his young son was fully returned, and it was with the most reverent heed that Rameses, on his accession, carried out and completed all that his father had begun. In Western Thebes Seti had founded a memorial sanctuary to his father's name, which he intended as his own burial-place. But 'he died,' says Rameses, 'and entered the realm of heaven and united himself with Ra, whilst this his house was being built. The gates showed a vacant place; all the works of stone and brick had yet to be raised, and all the writing and painting to be done.' The mummy of the king had, it seems, been placed meanwhile in his temple at Abydos. One morning it happened that, after celebrating a magnificent festival of Amen-Ra at Thebes, Rameses started at dawn of day for his new and favourite capital in the Delta.[1] The royal ships, it is said, threw their brightness on the river. Orders had been given for the journey down the stream, but on reaching the canal that led to Abydos the young king gave directions

[1] See on p. 162.

to turn aside thither that he might 'behold the face of his father and offer sacrifice.' But on arriving, he was much struck by the general dilapidation of the tombs, and the marks of careless neglect on every side. 'Nothing had been built up,' he said, 'by the son for the father, though he should have been careful to preserve it according to his expectations, since its possessor had taken flight to heaven. But not one son had renewed the memorial of his father who rested in the grave.' On examining his own father's temple, he found evidence not only of neglect but of dishonesty. 'The revenues had failed, the servants of the temple had taken, without exception, whatever had come in for themselves.' Consequently the columns were not raised on their bases, the statues lay prostrate on the ground. Rameses forthwith called together the princes, the captains and the architects, and after their prostrations and flattering speeches were ended he addressed them. After speaking of the state of things he had found at Abydos, he went on to say: 'The most beautiful thing to behold, the best thing to hear, is a child with a thankful breast, whose heart beats for his father. When I was but a little boy I attained to the supremacy. The lord of all himself nourished and brought me up; he gave over to me the land. I sat on his lap as a child, and he presented me publicly to the people, saying, " I will have him crowned king, for my desire is to behold his glory whilst I am yet alive. Place the royal diadem upon his brow. May he restore order and set up again that which has fallen into ruin. May he care for the people, the inhabitants of the land." Thus graciously did he speak out of his tender love towards me. Therefore will I do what is fitting and good for Seti Menephtah.[1] I will renew his memory. I will not neglect his tomb, as children are accustomed to do who do not remember their parents. I will complete it because I am lord of the country. I will take care of it because it is right and seemly.' He is answered with profuse flatteries, and is assured that none but he and Horus, son of Isis, imagine and perform such things. The king then appoints the following song for his own honour and in his father's memory:—

[1] Or Meri-en-Ptah, Seti's crown name, meaning 'Beloved of Ptah.'

'Awake, lift up thy face towards heaven; behold the sun, O my father, thou who hast become like God. Here am I who will make thy name to live. I myself, I myself am come here to build thy temple near to that of Unnefer,[1] the eternal king.'

Rameses proceeds to tell of all his gifts and rich endowments, and then addresses his father thus :—

'Thou hast entered into the realm of heaven. Thou art in the company of Ra. Thou art united with the moon and stars. Thou restest in the deep like those who dwell with Unnefer the eternal king. When the sun ariseth thou dost behold its splendour: when he sinketh down to rest, thou art in his train. Thou enterest within the secret house, and remainest in the company of the gods. Speak thou to Ra and to Unnefer with a heart full of love, that he may grant long years and feasts of jubilee unto King Rameses. Well will it be for thee that I should reign for a long time, for thou wilt be honoured by a good son who remembers his father.'

In answer to this invocation Seti appears and promises all that the heart of a king could desire, and more especially the length of days entreated by his son.

Long life was certainly appointed to King Rameses, who reigned for 67 years. Whilst

---

[1] The Good Being, *i.e.* Osiris.

still a youth he was summoned to serious conflict. Not only had the Syrian princes again risen, but the powerful and civilised nation of the Kheta had prepared to put forth all its strength against its mighty rival. Their country lay north of Syria, and their dominion extended eastward over a part of Mesopotamia, and westward to the coast of Asia Minor. Seti had encountered them, but although he claimed a great victory, he had found it advisable immediately afterwards to conclude a treaty and to return home. Khetasir, king of the Kheta, encouraged perhaps by the extreme youth of Seti's successor, had formed a strong confederacy against Egypt, and placed himself at its head. Besides his Syrian and Phœnician allies, he had called together the inhabitants of Mesopotamia on the east, and of the towns on the sea-coast, including, some have imagined, a contingent from Ilium,[1] as yet unbesieged of Greek, and unknown in song. The Egyptian forces reached Kadesh and pitched their camp in its neighbourhood.

The scenes of this campaign are made very

[1] The identification of the name is but doubtful.

real and living to us, being painted and sculptured in full detail on the walls of the Theban temples, and its chief episode is immortalised in the heroic poem of Pentaur. We see the Egyptian camp in the form of a square, with a temporary wall of enclosure, formed by piled up shields; servants are resting, asses are wandering about; there too is the lion of Rameses, the famous beast who accompanied him in his campaigns, and whose name was Semem-kheftu-ef: 'Tearer to pieces of his enemies.' The king's tent is seen, and near it is the shrine of the god. An inscription duly informs us: 'This is the first legion of Amen, who bestows victory on King Rameses. Pharaoh is with it. It is pitching its camp.'

Another picture gives us an important episode. The inscription tell us: 'This is the arrival of the spies of Pharaoh. They are bringing two spies of the Kheta before the king. They are beating them to make them declare where the king of the Kheta is.' For the plain fact was that the Egyptians were very much at a loss. Not long before two men had come into the camp, professing themselves to be leaders of the Shasu, who were wishing to desert the cause of the Kheta and to join the Egyptian army; for the king of the Kheta was far away, and was remaining in the country of the Khilibu for fear of the Egyptians. Rameses, it is not unlikely, was flattered by this tribute to the terror inspired by his very name; at any rate he believed their story too easily, and set out at once with slender forces in a north-westerly direction, leaving the main body to follow more leisurely. But at this juncture the two spies mentioned in the inscription were captured, and from them was extorted the confession that the Kheta were not by any means far off, but were at that moment lying in ambush close at hand, had horses and riders in great number, and all implements of war, and were 'more in number than the sands of the sea.' Anger swelled high in the breast of the young king; he called together the leaders and captains, and bitterly upbraided them for their neglect and carelessness. 'You have been telling me every day that the enemy are far away in the country of the Khilibu, and now, hear what these men say. Bring up our forces to the attack—they are close at our side.' But meanwhile the king of the Kheta had fallen suddenly upon the main body of the Egyptian army, who were following the advanced guard slowly and in careless security, and had taken them completely by surprise. They gave way and fell back upon the road that led to the place where the king was stationed with his advanced guard. But 'when Pharaoh saw this he was wroth; he seized his armour and appeared like unto the god of war in his hour. He mounted his chariot and rushed forth alone. None was with him. He rushed upon the foe and cast them down, and subdued the people before him. Then did the king of the Kheta lift up his hands in supplication.'

The scene is a favourite one, and is depicted more than once. We see the orderly masses of the Kheta in contrast to their less regular and less warlike allies. We see the heroic onslaught of the king, and the desperate encounter of the chariots on the plain of the Orontes. The Khetan chariots are beheld overthrown and hurled into the river, where the horsemen are confusedly struggling. One prince is being dragged out and held with his head hanging down, and we learn 'This is the King of Khilibu; his warriors are raising him up after Pharaoh has thrown him into the water.'

Such was the battle of Kadesh, in which it is evident that the Egyptian army, after having been brought by bad generalship to the brink of destruction, was saved from ruin by the desperate valour and personal prowess of Rameses himself. It is this exploit that is celebrated by the poet Pentaur two years later in such glowing poetic hyperbole:—

'He arose like unto Mentu, the god of war, and put speed to his horses, and urged on his steeds,—named "Triumph in Thebes," and "Mut[1] is content." None dared follow his headlong assault. He was alone and none other with him. And lo! he was encircled by the Khetan host; 2500 chariots were around him, and countless hosts cut off the way behind. On each chariot three men stood, and all were massed together man to man.'

The king now speaks :—

'Not a prince, not a captain was by me. My chiefs and knights had failed. No man was there to take my part against the foe. O Amen, my father, I

---

[1] The 'Divine Mother,'—worshipped at Thebes with Amen-Ra.

know thee; where art thou? Has ever a father forgotten his son? Thy precepts, thy will have I ever denied? has ought I have done been apart from thee? These hosts of the foe, what are they to thee! Amen can humble the imperious and proud. To thee I built temples and offered rich gifts. The wealth of the nations I laid at thy feet. Lo! I am alone, and none other is with me. I called on my soldiers, and none heard my cry. More to me is thy power than myriads of men—than thousand times thousand arrayed for the war. On thee, father Amen, on thee do I call!

'In far-off Hermonthis my prayer was heard. He stood by my side. "Lo! I am come! Rameses Meriamen,[1] thy prayer has been heard. I *am* more to thee than thousand times thousand. And the brave heart I love—my blessing is his. Nor can ought that I will of accomplishment fail."

'Then I rose up like Mentu and smote down the foe. A terror seized them and none dared fight. No man could shoot nor grasp the spear. Headlong they plunged into the stream like the crocodile. Still stood the King of Kheta to behold King Rameses, for—"He was alone, none other with him." Once more did he attack with all his power, but I rushed upon them like a flame of fire and slew them where they stood. Each man cried unto his fellow, saying: "No mortal man is he who is against us. It is Set the mighty—'tis the god of war. Whoso draws near him his hand drops, nor can he grasp the bow or spear." I called upon my foot and horse: "Take

---

[1] Crown name, meaning 'beloved of Amen.'

heart—be firm—behold my victory." I was alone, but Amen was beside me.'

The whole poem is too long to be given here, but we learn that when at length the terror-stricken forces rallied upon seeing the victory of the king and beholding the multitude of corpses, they approached with adulation and flattery, extolling the hero to the skies. No wonder that his reply is stern :—

'The king spake and said : " O my captains and soldiers who have *not* fought! of what profit is all your devotion? Which of you has done his duty before his king? Who ever did for you what I did? and now have ye altogether failed me; none stood by to help me in the battle. Shame upon my horse and foot! shame more than words can say! As for my horses, they indeed were with me, and upheld me when I was alone amid the raging foe. Henceforth shall they eat food before me in my palace for ever.'

Next day the battle was resumed with fury, and at the close the Kheta sued for peace, which Rameses, apparently, was glad enough to grant. Accepting their submission he returned to Egypt 'joyful and glad at heart.'

A hearty welcome was accorded to the conqueror throughout Egypt, but nowhere was he so warmly received as in his favourite seat

RAMESES THE GREAT.
FROM A SCULPTURE IN THE BRITISH MUSEUM.

San-Tanis, better known to us as Zoan. In the early days of the monarchy this had been an important city and an emporium of trade. It stood on one of the arms of the Nile, and was not far from the eastern frontier of the Delta. The Hyksos kings had occupied it soon after their invasion; they often resided there, and under them it attained great splendour and importance. After their expulsion it was neglected, nor did it come again into prominence until the days of Rameses, who almost rebuilt it, and under whom it became one of the most magnificent of the great cities of Egypt. It was known as Pa-Ramessu, the 'city of Rameses,' and we are fortunate in possessing a description of it by an Egyptian writer, written apparently in prospect of the king's triumphal entry: 'I came to the city of Rameses Meri-amen. Beautiful is she exceedingly. Thebes itself is not comparable unto her—the secret of happiness is here. Her meadows are full of all things fair and good, daily producing abundance of food; the pools are full of fish, and the lakes swarm with waterfowl; the fields are green with verdure; the melons are sweet as honey. The barns and threshing-floors are full of wheat and barley, heaped up even unto heaven; herbs of all kinds abound in the gardens; there the apple-tree blooms, the vine, the citron, and the fig-tree. Sweet is the wine like honey. The canal yields salt, the lake of Paher, natron (soda). The ships come and go daily, and there is plenty without stint. Gladness dwells in Pa-Ramessu, and happy is he whose habitation is therein. The lowly ones are like unto the great. They all unite to say: "Come and let us celebrate the heavenly and the earthly festivals!" The people of the marsh land bring lilies, and from Pshenhor come the crimson-tinted flowers of the pools. The maidens of the "conqueror's city" are adorned as for a day of festivity. They stand at the doors, and their hands are filled with flowers and garlands on the morning of the day when King Rameses Meri-amen, the war-god upon earth, makes his entry. All flock together, neighbour with neighbour; each man bringing his petition.

'Sweet is the wine of the conqueror's city. Cider and delicious drinks abound. Sweet song by the women of the school of Memphis resounds; joy is in every heart. All are as one to celebrate the praises of this god—even of King Rameses Meri-amen, the war-god of the world.'

In the early part of his reign, Rameses was engaged in more than one warlike enterprise, but none ever created so much excitement, or so fascinated the popular imagination as that of the first campaign by the Orontes at Kadesh, which was celebrated with such true poetic licence in Pentaur's epic song. Never, indeed, were the records of any sovereign's life and victories so blazoned abroad as those of King Rameses; the walls of the temples in Egypt and in Nubia are covered with inscriptions, paintings, and sculptures belonging to this reign. One while we see him in what appears most inglorious warfare—trampling down a crowd of negroes, who are represented as pigmies, and over whom he is driving his chariot of war. Some have escaped, and are flying in hot haste towards their homes, represented by the little huts like bee-hives, such as are still common in Africa. A little child rushes forward to greet them, but the mother stands still, holding up her hands in an attitude of despair; a little farther off another negress is seen with a pot over the fire, which she is carefully watching that it may be ready for the returning soldier. She does not yet see the boy who is even at that moment running up to bring the fatal news. At another time the king is seen seated upon his throne in state receiving the negro tribute—giraffes, oxen, ostriches, and several monkeys appear in the drawing. Or he is receiving prisoners brought in by his generals, whilst Semem-kheftu-ef, the 'Tearer to pieces of his enemies,' is lying quietly at the foot of the throne.

On the walls of the colossal temple of Abu-simbel in Nubia, is a whole series of tableaux pertaining to the life of Rameses II. There is one striking bas-relief representing three of his sons following him in a headlong charge upon the battle-field. The three princes speed on, each in his chariot, side by side, and each of them is attended by a charioteer, who carries a large shield for their defence. But Rameses himself is alone, in the fore-front. Not even a charioteer stands beside him. The reins are

HALL IN THE GREAT TEMPLE AT IPSAMBUL.

fastened round his waist, whilst he bends the bow firmly with his hands. Above his head flies the hawk, the bird of Ra, ensign of the protection of the god. In another bas-relief, he is pausing for a moment, and checking his steeds. Semem-kheftu-ef is running by his side like a dog.

These are only two illustrations out of the multitude carved with spirit and fidelity upon the interior of the great temple hewn in the sandstone rock at Abu-simbel, in Nubia, which, even in its present condition, excites a wonder that is akin to awe. In front of the entrance stand four colossal statues of the king seated on his throne, each of which is 66 feet in height. The face is grandly represented; a calm, haughty repose marks the features, and the placid, if not scornful, smile so characteristic of the king rests upon his lips—accustomed to speak in accents of command from early childhood and on to extreme old age. Close by is a smaller temple erected by queen Nefertari, the loved wife of his early manhood, in honour of her lord. Within its walls we may see family groups sculptured—the king in the prime of manhood, his beautiful young wife, and her children. An inscription tells us that—'To the sovereign of the two lands, son of the Sun, lord of crowns, Rameses Meri-amen, his loving lady, queen, and princess Nefertari, has built a temple at Abu by the waters. Grant him life for evermore!' In the great temple, Nefertari is only once depicted; here the children are grown up, and the sons follow their father to the battle. Rameses himself is older, the glow and ardour of early years have given way to the placidity and repose of later life, when his wars and his victories were over; for, though renowned as a conqueror, the greater part of his long reign passed by in peace. Nefertari herself does not seem to have lived long, and Rameses apparently was married two or three times; his last wife (so far as we can gather) was a foreign princess, whose hand was the pledge of lasting friendship and alliance between the two leading nations of the day.[1]

The proposal came from Khetasir, king of the Kheta. A tacit respect for each other

[1] For the substance of this and of the foregoing paragraphs, I have been much indebted to *Nile Gleanings* and to its very interesting illustrations.

seems to have prevented a renewal of the war which had opened with the battle of Kadesh, but Khetasir wished to go further. Between the two great and civilised nations lay the seething and restless masses of the Canaanitish tribes. Powerful kings had ruled ere this in Elam and in Mesopotamia, and might rule there again. No worse policy could be conceived than that of mutual rivalry and strife between Egypt and Kheta. An envoy brought to King Rameses a copy of the proposed treaty written on a silver tablet, and on its acceptance Khetasir himself came to Egypt and was received in all state by Rameses at the city of Zoan, where the treaty was duly ratified, and the King of Egypt received the hand of the Khetan princess in token of lasting amity and goodwill. 'Peace and good brotherhood shall be between us for ever,' so runs the treaty; 'he shall be at peace with me and I with him for ever. The children's children of the King of Kheta shall be in good brotherhood and peace with the children's children of Rameses Meri-amen, the great ruler of Egypt. The King of Kheta shall not invade Egypt, nor the great ruler of Egypt invade Kheta, to carry away anything from it. If any enemy shall come against the land of Rameses he shall send to the ruler of Kheta, who shall help him to smite the enemy.' All the gods of both countries are solemnly called upon to witness to this treaty, and to visit with dire penalties any infraction of its provisions. A further clause of 'extradition' is added, but it is humanely stipulated that any refugees given up in fulfilment of its demands shall not be punished with severity in any way. The treaty thus made was well and truly kept. The marriage of Rameses with the daughter of his ally is recorded in the rock-temple of Abusimbel. 'The Prince of Kheta, clad in the dress of his country, himself conducted the bride to his son-in-law. After the marriage had taken place the young wife, as queen, received the Egyptian name of Urma-Neferura.' Not only did all hostilities cease henceforth between the two great empires, but a calm ensued throughout Syria, where the tribal kings could no longer look for support to their powerful neighbours. It seems as if Rameses quietly allowed his claims to supremacy in Mesopotamia to lapse; and the Phœnicians were not a warlike race, but, as a rule, were ready to acknowledge the supremacy of a stronger nation so long as they could pursue their commerce and gain wealth at their ease.

It is possible, then, that thirty or forty years of peace may have remained for King Rameses, and his time and energies were devoted to architectural, instead of warlike, achievements. He lived to be at least eighty years of age, and survived twelve of his sons, being succeeded by the thirteenth, Menephtah.

Behind the Libyan hills, which encircle the plain of Western Thebes, is a wild and desolate valley. At its entrance stood a beautiful temple, begun by Seti I. in memory of his father, and completed by Rameses. In the hills surrounding this lonely valley (called by the Arabs *Biban el Moluk*, Tombs of the Kings) were the burial-places of the nineteenth and twentieth dynasties. In another and an equally dreary valley were the tombs of the queens and princesses of the royal house. Their fate has been a sad one, for the graves have been ruthlessly searched and the mummies torn to pieces in hopes of plunder, and when all of value had been taken, the dishonoured remains of the queens and princesses appear to have been replaced, without care or ceremony, in their rock-hewn tombs, and burned in heaps. The fire thus kindled has calcined the walls of the tombs and sorely damaged the paintings and inscriptions. A few only have escaped; amongst them is a very perfectly preserved portrait of Tai-ti, the beautiful wife of Amen-hotep III.[1]

The care taken in inspecting, and from time to time removing, the bodies of the kings prevented such wholesale destruction; but little could Thothmes or Rameses have dreamt of the destiny that should befall them. Discovered at last in their final hiding-place, their mummies, together with others of earlier and later date, were conveyed down the sacred stream, and, by a strange irony of fate, are now exhibited amongst other curiosities in a museum.

[1] See *Nile Gleanings*.

Discovery of Mummies at Deir el' Bahari, near Thebes.

CHAPTER XI.

Thebes; its People, Temples, and Tombs—Close of the Nineteenth Dynasty.

In an inscription on the walls of the rock-temple at Abu-simbel, Rameses is represented as saying to the god Ptah, 'I have cared for the land to create for thee a new Egypt, such as it existed in the olden times,' and he specially mentions the splendid sanctuary he had built for that deity in Memphis. And not at Memphis alone, but everywhere throughout the land, from the city of Rameses in the north to the wonderful rock-temples of the south, we can see the magnificent traces left by the hand of this mighty sovereign. In Thebes itself, he added a grand court to the temple of Luxor founded by Amenhotep III. of the preceding dynasty. This temple was connected by an avenue of sphinxes with the still more magnificent 'great Temple of Amen,' the foundation of which had been laid by Amenemhat I., not long after the close of the civil wars, and before the Hyksos invasion.

However the Egyptian temples might differ in size or splendour, the idea and plan were alike—so that it has been said, 'If you have seen one temple, you have seen all.' A wall of enclosure surrounded the precincts, which were adorned with trees, flowers, and artificial lakes. The temple itself was approached by an avenue of sphinxes. Before the entrance stood obelisks and colossal statues. On either side of the gateway rose the pylons—massive towers, broader at the base than at the summit; they were covered with pictorial and sculptured representations of the great events of the day, and above them rose the tall masts of cedar wood, whence floated the gay streamers on days of festival and rejoicing. Passing through between the pylons, a vast court was entered, surrounded by columns and open to the sky. Beyond were halls, the roofs supported on pillars, and in these the light glimmered but faintly amidst the forest of majestic columns. Each hall or court was of less size than the one

Temple and Garden.

M

before it, and the innermost sanctuary was small, dark, and mysterious in its solemn obscurity. Here was the sacred shrine (containing some hidden emblem or image of the god), which on solemn occasions was brought out and carried in procession through the city or down the river. These shrines or arks are seen depicted in brightly coloured tints on the bas-reliefs. The sacred bark is standing on an altar, which is covered by a red cloth. On two lesser altars stand flowers and vessels for libation or for incense. In the centre of the boat is the ark itself, a sort of chest partially veiled, in which is for ever hidden the mystic symbol of the god. In the bark are small images of men kneeling in adoration, and immense artificial lotus and papyrus flowers. Tall banners or sun-screens stand behind, ready to be carried in solemn state in the processions. On the prow of the boat is the sacred hawk, and behind it a sphinx, emblem of the king. Underneath are the shafts on which it rests when it is taken from the altar and borne on the shoulders of the priests. Not only the mystic shrine itself, but statues or images of the gods were frequently carried in procession with music, song, and universal rejoicings—queens and princesses deeming it an honour to take part, carrying the sistrum or musical instrument used in the service of the gods. As a rule the people probably were allowed only to enter the vast outer court, kings and priests alone penetrating to the interior recesses, where sacrifices were offered and incense ascended in clouds. Sublimity and mystery were the ideas expressed in these Egyptian temples,[1] with their vast halls and shrouded recesses. Comparatively little thought and care were expended on private residences, which were simple and unpretending. The poor were content if they had shelter from the heat and a place of storage for their goods. In the construction of the houses belonging to the richer classes the leading idea was still protection from the heat, so that the windows were small, and had wooden shutters. The walls inside were decorated with paintings, and even the outside was gaily tinted by this colour-loving people, who coloured

---

[1] In one hall, forming only a *part* of the temple in which it stands, the Cathedral of Notre Dame, at Paris, could stand without touching the walls!

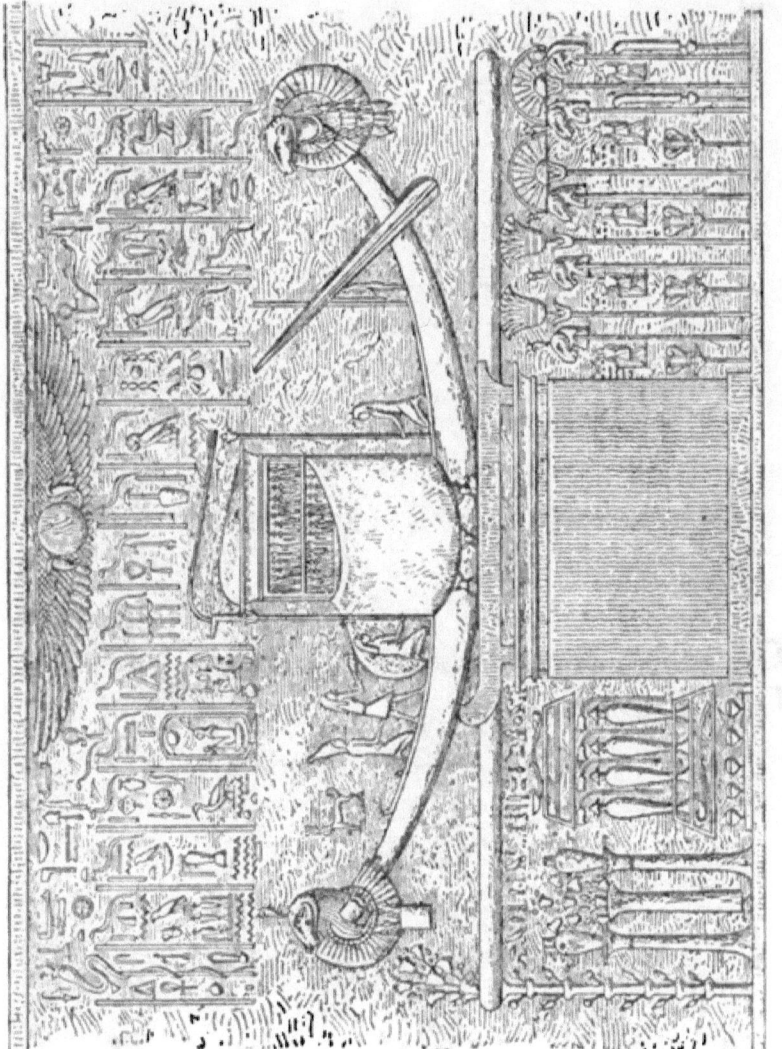

The Sacred Ark.

everything that would admit of it. On the flat roofs of the houses much time was spent, as also in the beautiful gardens watered by small canals in the absence of rain, and adorned with fish-ponds, trees, and abundance of flowers. A late Greek writer goes so far as to say that 'flowers of every sort grew all the year round, and that roses and violets especially grew at all seasons.' Be that as it may, the love of the Egyptians for flowers was very great. Flowers are used on all occasions—in social banquets they are in profusion, and they are never wanting in the funeral solemnities; they furnish both decorations for the rooms and houses and oblations for the gods.

The house was generally built round a court-yard planted with trees and refreshed by a fountain. In the country the farm-yards and sheds were at some distance from the dwelling-house; the cattle were tied up at feeding-time to rings placed in rows, and were often fed by the hand. Around the country-houses were orchards of fig-trees, together with sycamore, peach, pomegranate, date, olive, and almond trees, besides others of names and kinds unknown. Monkeys were sometimes employed in gathering the fruit, and we see from the pictures that they did not fail to help themselves at the same time. Our museums show us the tables and chairs of all sorts that were used by the Egyptians—common chairs, camp-stools, and arm-chairs of elegant workmanship, sometimes of ebony inlaid with ivory. There are the double chairs where the master and mistress of the house sat when receiving their guests—couches, footstools, carpets which served as bedding, and the wooden rests on which the head was placed at night. Children's toys of all kinds may be seen, and a variety of musical instruments; for music was much studied, and was employed not only in the service of the temples, but in the social gatherings of the people, which seem to have been frequent. But both music and dancing on such occasions appear to have been performed for the amusement of the guests, who are themselves only lookers-on. Buffoons also exhibited, who seem generally to have been negroes; they are oddly dressed in a bit of bullock's hide, with the tail attached and tags hanging like beads from their

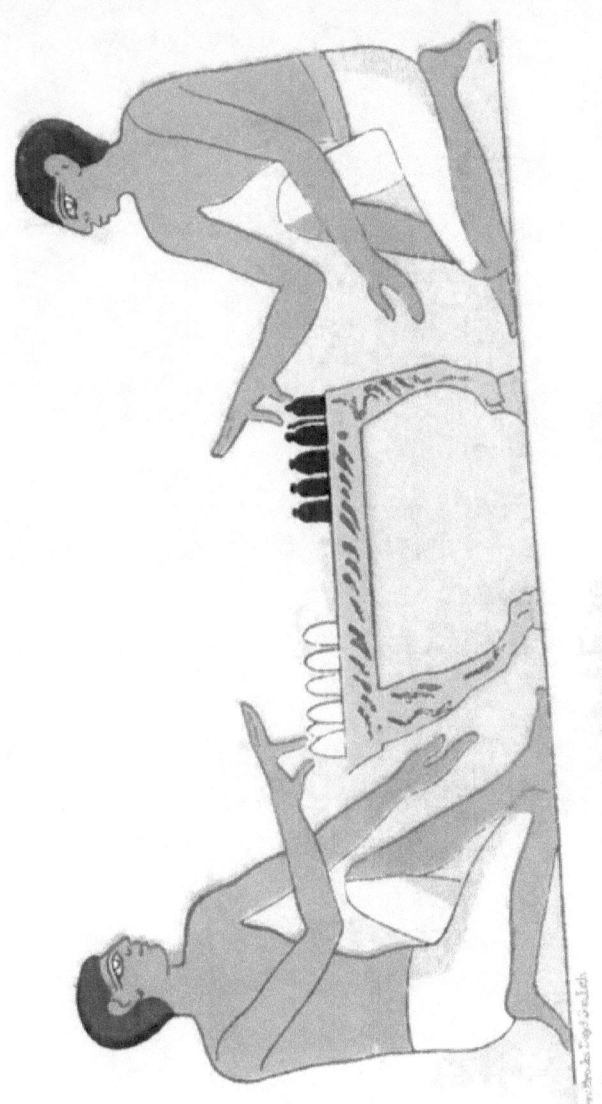

PLAYING AT DRAUGHTS.

elbows. The chase was a most popular amusement, and besides stags, hares, etc., there was the exciting sport of hunting wilder beasts, wolves, jackals, and lions in the desert lands. Fowling and fishing were common pastimes. We do not meet with the least trace of anything approaching to gladiatorial shows; such scenes would have been abhorrent to the Egyptian nature. Amongst indoor games we see odd and even—*mora* (a guessing game), draughts, and others unknown to us. Athletic games and outdoor exercises were encouraged amongst children, and there was a great fondness for playing ball, especially amongst the girls, who attained great skill in the exercise, sometimes catching two or three balls at a time. There was great freedom in social intercourse, and women mixed in society quite as freely as men.[1]

The Egyptians have, in fact, painted their social life for us themselves in fullest detail, whether it is the king standing proudly in his war-chariot and striking down his foe, or the potter patiently turning his wheel; the priest

---

[1] For the foregoing particulars and some of the following, see Sir J. Gardner Wilkinson's *Ancient Egyptians*.

officiating in the temple rites, or the fisherman directing his tiny craft upon the river. We see the baker kneading the dough with his feet, and the flat loaves being carried round to the customers; the shoemaker, sitting on his three-legged stool, is busy fashioning the leather sandal; spinning-wheel and loom are producing the 'fine linen' of Egypt, and the needle is skilful in beautiful embroidered work. The pottery is of varied and graceful form, the jewellery of exquisite workmanship. Glass is fashioned, and so is brightly tinted porcelain ware; veneering too is practised with much skill.

We may picture to ourselves the active life and gay animation that reigned in the streets of the mighty city that had grown up around the great temples of Amen, or, on the broad waters of the stream, the scene of constant traffic, where boats laden with merchandise, fishing vessels, and gay-looking pleasure-boats went to and fro in ceaseless motion. The Nile valley is of unusual breadth on both sides of the river here, and forms a sort of amphitheatre closed in by mountain ranges of varied outlines.

It seemed hidden away out of the invader's track, the 'great city' in all her imperial beauty, *Apu*, the 'city of thrones,' or *Nu*, 'the city,' as her people called her of old. The sky is of a deeper blue than in the northern part of the country; and in spite of ceaseless sunshine the fields are clothed in richest verdure. Here, as everywhere, light and colour reign, the shadows themselves are luminous, so radiant is the light, and the colour harmonies of the sunset are thus described:—

'The western horizon is a furnace of molten gold, the stems and foliage of the palm trees are likewise gold, and through this dazzling glow the purple tints of the hills can just be perceived. The sky and the Nile become in turn rose-coloured and violet, like the colour of an amethyst; then the light dies away.'[1]

Let us follow the western sun, and cross the stream, leaving behind us the life and animation of the great city. Here, too, is a city—Western Thebes[2]—and its streets contain a population vaster far than that upon the other side. But

[1] Ampère, *Voyage en Egypte et Nubie*.
[2] Thebes was indeed always considered as two cities. Homer makes it plural, and it has ever since been so—*Thebæ*.

all is silent here; no man buys or sells or joins in festive mirth. It is the City of the Dead. Here lie in countless numbers the embalmed bodies of those who have passed away generation after generation: kings and priests—men, women, children—the freeman and the slave. The hills encircling the plain are pierced and honeycombed in all directions with passages and tombs. Here are the 'eternal dwellings' of those who on the other side inhabit 'hostelries' as strangers of a day. And far more thought and care are bestowed upon those than upon these.[1] There are large common tombs, in which the bodies of the poor lie ranged side by side. And there are the funeral chambers of the rich, with their sculptured façades, whence winding galleries lead into the heart of the rock. Shafts are sunk, false passages that lead nowhere are constructed. Everything is done that human ingenuity can suggest, if only the body hidden there might never be seen or handled again.[2] Nor is the silent city of the

[1] The Greek writer Diodorus Siculus says: 'The Egyptians call their houses hostelries, since they can enjoy them for a brief space only; whereas their tombs are the eternal dwelling-places of the future.'

[2] For some parts of the description of the cities of Thebes, see Karl Oppel's *Land der Pyramiden*.

dead without its stately palaces and temples. The two colossal twin statues of Amenhotep III. sit there upon the plain, and behind them is his magnificent temple. A little farther is the Ramesseum, a great temple erected by Rameses 'to his name,' and to the memory of his ancestors, marvellous for size and splendour. In the face of the limestone cliff to the north-west arises the stately terraced temple of Queen Hatasu, and not far off is the narrow gorge leading to the desolate valley of the 'tombs of the kings.'

The priests attached to the service of these temples must have lived in the neighbourhood and kept up intercourse with the world outside, and in Western Thebes were the dwellings of all those whose business was with the bodies of the dead,—of those who first opened the corpse, who were reckoned ceremonially unclean, and of those who skilfully embalmed and bandaged it afterwards. Not a day could have passed on which some company of mourners, rich or poor, did not land—their 'dark freight, a vanished life;' whilst now and again a gorgeous funeral procession wound its way through the narrow defile, bearing beneath a funeral tent of exquisite workmanship the body of some prince or princess of the Pharaoh's house to its last long home in the western hills.

One day in the year (as we should say, on All Souls' Day) the family and friends of the departed assembled amidst the dead. On that day the silent city was alive and Eastern Thebes deserted. All day long boats of every sort plied to and fro, and the western plain was covered with vast crowds bringing flowers and garlands and funeral gifts. Within the funeral chambers, richly and brightly adorned with paintings and sculptures, the family groups assembled, the scenes around awakening vivid associations of the past. The sound of human talk was heard, and the voice of minstrelsy and song. The feast is spread, and here, says a modern writer[1] who has vividly described the whole scene, the assembled family in their social union 'remembered their departed ones as if they were travellers who had found happiness in a distant land, and whom they might hope to see once again sooner or later.' In

[1] Ebers, in his Egyptian novel of the time of Rameses II., *Uarda*.

fact, at the feast thus spread the dead were always looked upon as guests, although unseen, and were addressed in the festive songs. One of these songs, known as the 'Lay of the Harper,' has been preserved. It is in memory of a priest of Amen named Neferhotep; part is to the following effect :—

'Truly is he now at rest, faithfully his work fulfilled. Men go hence since days of Ra. Youths arise to take their place.

'Holy prophet,[1] keep the feast-day! Fragrant oil, delicious balsam, lo, we bring, and flowery wreaths twine we round her breast and arms: Her thy sister dearly loved, resting ever by thy side.

'Lift the song and strike the chords, in the presence chamber here! Leave all idle cares behind, and be mindful, Man, of joy, till thy day for going hence, when the traveller findeth rest, in the silence-loving land.

'Holy prophet, keep the feast-day! Perfect thou and pure of heart. They who lived have passed away—are as though they had not been. Thy soul dwells amongst them there, by the sacred river's side, drinking of the crystal stream.

'Holy prophet, keep the feast-day! Neferhotep, pure of heart . . . Nought might all his works avail, to add one moment to his years. . . .

'Mind thee of the day, O man, when thou too

---

[1] Addressed to the departed seer.

must take thy way to the land whence none return. Good for thee then an honest life. For he who loveth Right is blest.

'Brave nor coward flee the grave. Proud and humble meet one fate. Give, then, freely, as 'tis meet. Isis will bless the good. Happy shall thine old age prove.'

The memorial chambers in which these feasts were celebrated were adorned with pictures and carving representing the familiar scenes of daily life, but in the gloomy recesses beyond mystic and awful scenes are depicted. The representations of the gods, not often met with in earlier times, had now become common and familiar; and so does Amenti itself cease to be the 'hidden' world, and the scenes and events of the life after death appear in visible though mystic shape. The Egyptian from of old believed in the judgment before Osiris, but now it was depicted. The heart is seen weighed in the balance; Osiris is enthroned as judge; Thoth records the result.[1] The trials that await the spirit take bodily form as foul and hideous monsters that must be encoun-

[1] I am not sure at how early a date the judgment scene is depicted in any existing funeral papyri; but I believe there is no doubt that neither that nor any 'other world' scene occurs in the tombs of the earlier dynasties, so far as they are yet known.

The Weighing of Actions.

tered and overcome; good and guardian powers appear as star-crowned genii of light; and for the impure spirit the furnace of purifying fire is kindled, behind which stands a figure holding in his hand the emblem of the purity that must be won.

Nor is it the conflicts and triumphs of the human spirit alone that are portrayed, but the conflicts and triumphs of the gods themselves. We read in a very ancient chapter of the sacred book: 'I am Ra in his first supremacy—the great god, self-existing. There was a battle-field of the gods prepared when I spake.' Later on a more tangible shape and form is given to this great battle. In the tomb of Seti I. we may see it all in allegory and mystic symbol. Here is depicted in a series of tableaux the 'passage of the Sun through the hours of the day and of the night,' *i.e.* of the visible and invisible world, beholding and ruling all, both mortal and immortal. Ra in his bark, the 'ancient and unknown One in his mystery,' accompanied by gods and spirits, finds the 'field of battle prepared.' The serpent of evil, Apepi, lies in wait, hidden beneath the waves of the celestial rivers—the ether. After a hard struggle he is drawn out and destroyed, and the heavenly bark disappears in peace behind the western horizon, received by the mother goddess Nut.[1] A hymn addressed to Ra, 'Lord of the horizon,' celebrates his triumph: 'Thou awakenest, triumphant and blessed One, thou who comest in radiance and travellest in thy disk! Thy divine bark[2] speeds on, blest by thy mother Nut each day; thy foes fall as thou turnest thy face to the western heaven. Glad are the mariners of thy bark; Ra hath quelled his impious foe, he striketh down the evil one, thou breakest his strength, casting him into the fire that encircleth in its season the children of wickedness.'

An eminent writer who has devoted himself to the study of ancient religions says:—' In spite of the abundance of materials, in spite of the ruins of temples and numberless statues and half-deciphered papyri—I must confess that we have not yet come very near the

[1] Notice the similarity of thought underlying this myth and that of Osiris and Set.
[2] This idea of a sacred bark appears also in the form assigned to the sacred shrine, p. 177.

beatings of the heart that gave life to all this strange and mysterious grandeur."¹ This is only what might be expected; for the symbolism of any religion is apt to assume an unmeaning and often a grotesque appearance in the eyes of men professing another faith, and no religion was ever so pervaded by symbolism as that of ancient Egypt. Symbols are not, in any sense, works of art; they are never chosen for intrinsic worth or beauty,² and are valueless, excepting for the sake of some association of idea, which led to their selection. They are intended to represent, but not seldom also to veil, thoughts and mysteries that cannot be uttered in language, or *expressed* in any form or image. But in all religions there is a tendency to separate the symbol from the thought, and this, carried to its fullest extent, ends in idolatry; the mere

---

¹ Max Müller, *Science of Religion*.

² Take in illustration the symbols on any national flag. There is no intrinsic beauty in three coloured stripes, or in the grotesque figures of lions rampant. Yet for the sake of the nation of which they have become symbolic, men will die sooner than surrender the banners on which they are depicted. It is the same with the symbols of rival religions. How fierce the conflict waged by Saracen and Christian beneath the respective symbols of the Crescent and the Cross!

symbol seems to the ignorant and superstitious to be endowed with power and divine attributes, and becomes itself a god. That which gave the Egyptian religion an especially strange and even absurd aspect, in the eyes of Greek and Roman travellers of a later day, was its use of living symbols, *i.e.* of the sacred animals, which was then so excessive as to have become its prominent feature on first sight, and which led to idolatry of the most base and degraded kind.

There are a few traces of the existence of animal worship under the early dynasties; they are but few, however, and, so far as I am aware, no notice of sacred animals occurs between the age of Khufu and the reign of Rameses II. Nor are the gods depicted in the memorial chambers of the departed before the times of the eighteenth dynasty. Under Thothmes III., their figures are constantly met with, often with the head of the symbolic creature that was their emblem (see p. 119). The reason for the selection is often plain. The bull or the ram might denote undaunted strength and the protection of the weak, the hawk unerring sight, the crocodile terror, the scarabæus tender foresight and unwearied care for its offspring. And not only were the gods represented under the form of these and other objects, but the living animals themselves were symbolic and sacred. Each district had its own sacred animal, fed and tended with the devoutest care. Certain of them, however, attained to far greater celebrity than the rest—the Ram of Mendes; Mnevis, the bull sacred to Ra, at Heliopolis; and, above all, Apis, the bull sacred to Ptah, at Memphis. The eldest son of Rameses, named Khamus, who was governor of Memphis, was also high priest of Ptah, and more especially under his form or manifestation as Apis. It requires very little knowledge of human nature, and very little acquaintance with history, to feel assured that the crowds who gathered round these symbolic creatures would regard them with superstitious reverence, and that to not a few the animal would be no longer a symbol but a god.

Animal worship grew and developed immensely after the days of Rameses. At a later period we find Greek and Roman travellers noticing it with curiosity or **contempt**. Herodotus and Strabo saw the sacred crocodiles in the Fayoum, adorned with golden ornaments, and fed with the flesh of the **sacrifices**. Diodorus tells us of the furious wrath of Egyptian villagers against a Roman soldier who had killed a cat. The comic writers of Greece and the satirists of Rome made merry over these peculiar deities.

'You are never done laughing **every** day of your lives at the Egyptians,' says an **early** Christian writer to his heathen contemporaries. Philo, the Jewish philosopher of Alexandria, tells us that foreigners coming to Egypt knew not what to do for laughter at the divine animals, but that in the end they were themselves overpowered by the superstition. There were not wanting those who, acknowledging that the animals were **to be** regarded merely as symbolic, based their arguments against **the** custom on that very ground.[1] The days of

---

[1] The biographer of Apollonius of Tyana records the following conversation. 'The beasts and **birds**,' says Apollonius, 'may derive dignity from such representations, but the gods will lose theirs.' 'I think,' says his opponent, 'you slight our mode of worship before you have given it a fair examination. For surely what we are speaking of is wise, if anything Egyptian is so; the Egyptians do not venture to

foreign criticism were, however, as yet in the distant future when the kings of the nineteenth dynasty were on the throne.

The growth of animal worship seems to speak of degradation in the national religion, and there are not wanting at the same time evidences both of a decay in the national morality and of a decline in art. When art is required to work by the acre its productions are not likely to be distinguished by high excellence or exquisite finish. In the drawings of the time of Rameses the heads indeed are still good and the portraits characteristic, but the figures are ill-drawn in the extreme, and often most hastily finished off. Egyptian art suffered severely under the influence of certain fixed rules concerning the drawing and the proportion of figures. Under the earlier dynasties there are

give any form to their deities, they only give them in symbols which have an occult meaning, that renders them venerable.' Apollonius, however, is not convinced: he admits that the mind forms to itself an idea which it pictures better than any art can do, but he complains that the Egyptian custom takes from the gods the very power of appearing beautiful either to the eye or to the mind. Porphyry also regards the worship as symbolic; he says that 'under the semblance of animals the Egyptians worship the universal power which the gods have revealed in the various forms of living nature.' These quotations and those in the text are taken from Le Page Renouf's *Hibbert Lectures.*

signs of greater freedom of treatment than prevailed at a later period, when the conventional rules, which no one ventured to infringe, had checked the progress of all true art by putting a stop to its free exercise. This following of a stereotyped pattern, combined with the absence of perspective, gives the Egyptian drawings a very odd and stiff appearance. The portraiture remained excellent, and much spirit was often shown in the drawing of animals and in humorous scenes; indeed, the manner in which, in hieroglyphic writing, the individual character of an animal or bird is given in a few minute lines is quite wonderful. The graceful outline of their pottery, the exquisite workmanship of their jewellery, show how much true artistic power was there, had it only been allowed free scope. But there never was a nation that clung so tenaciously to fixed laws and forms. Their monarchy, their religion, lasted unchanged as no other has yet done;[1] the very fashion of their dress varied but little with the centuries, and their magnificent temples were built and rebuilt on the same scheme. But

---

[1] We may, perhaps, except the Chinese.

already, under the nineteenth dynasty, other influences were strongly at work. The Delta was full of foreign settlers, and the names of some of its cities were Semitic. Literature was affected, and the younger writers of the day were given to introducing Semitic words and phrases—just as an English or German author does with French. Whole bodies of mercenary troops were employed in the army under a special commander; others were used in the naval service, which was never very popular in Egypt, but which was becoming of more and more importance. Others again, not judged fit for these branches, were reduced to serfage, being employed in the service of the kings and of the temples, or in still harder bondage on the public buildings, in the quarries, or the mines. Many of these, we learn, were branded with the name of the god or master to whom they were assigned, and here we see at once the arising of that distrust and fear which always beset the ease of the owners of the slave. Slavery was universal in the ancient world, but in Egypt it had always worn a milder aspect than it ever assumed in any other country, unless it were Greece, much of whose early civilisation came from the land of the Nile. Even in the days of harsher servitude at which we have now arrived, there were no such hideous cruelties as we meet with in the blood-stained pages of Roman, Carthaginian, or American slavery. The Egyptian slave was well fed, and by the moral and religious code maltreatment of a slave was an offence. We do not know the legal code on this subject, but the moral tone is clearly shown in the confession every ruler had to make before Osiris: 'I have allowed no master to maltreat his slave.' But moral feeling can grow blunt, and maltreatment was not wanting in the days of Rameses II.

The Hebrew colony in Goshen, so warmly welcomed by the Hyksos kings, must have been regarded with distrust on the accession of the native dynasty, which 'knew not Joseph,' and had the utmost aversion for aught that was connected with the rulers he had served. Under Rameses, or one of his predecessors, the Hebrews had been reduced to cruel bondage; 'they built for Pharaoh treasure-cities, Pithom and Raamses."[1] Their future deliverer, rescued from death by a princess of the royal house,[2] must have spent many years at Zoan, the favourite residence of Rameses, which was close to the district of Goshen, and there he would have the opportunity at any moment of 'going out to his brethren and looking upon their burdens.'

Moses did not return from his exile during the lifetime of Rameses, but 'in *process of time*' that sovereign died.[3] On the accession of Menephtah the hardships of the people were intensified, but their deliverance was close at hand. There is no need to relate the familiar story of their marvellous escape, and of the pursuit, in which so many of the chosen chariots and horses of Menephtah perished.

[1] Recent investigation has identified Tel-el-Maschuta, a spot not far from the modern Ismailia, as the site of both the Pithom and the Succoth of the Old Testament; the former was the sacred, the latter the civil name of the city, which is thus shown to have been one of the store-cities built by the Israelites (Ex. i. 11), and also the first stage reached by them on their journey (Ex. xii. 37; xiii. 20). The word *Ar*, meaning storehouse, occurs in the inscription by which M. Naville first identified Pithom-Succoth.

[2] Generally supposed to have been a daughter of Rameses, but if Moses was eighty when he stood before the successor of that monarch, that would have been impossible.

[3] Ex. ii. 23. How well this incidental allusion coincides with the sixty-seven years' reign of Rameses II.!

No inscriptions or records have, as yet, been found relating to the long sojourn of the Israelites in Egypt, to the oppression, or to the exodus, though there can be little doubt that some of the highest interest might be brought to light were the exploration of the historic sites of the Delta undertaken in earnest.[1] The chief event recorded of the reign of Menephtah is connected with the western boundary. On the north-east the frontier district bristled with fortresses, where sentinels kept their daily and nightly watch. The great military route that started thence was well guarded, and a regular communication kept up with the Egyptian garrisons, which were still maintained in some parts of Syria. By the same road there was a constant commercial intercourse with Phœnicia, and probably also to some extent with the distant Khetan allies;—we find, at any rate, from an incidental allusion, that during a famine in that land, the lives of the people were saved by corn sent from Egypt at Menephtah's direction. But on the western

---

[1] Such an investigation has been recently undertaken by the *Egypt Exploration Fund*. The extent to which it may be carried depends entirely on the means placed at its disposal.

frontier, the limits were not so definite. There was less anxiety and less watchfulness. Whilst the utmost thought and vigilance had been exerted in the north-east, the west had been left practically undefended. Whole districts had long been harassed by the inroads of the Libyan tribes, and cultivation had ceased. The invaders had even gained a firm footing in some places, and had ventured to settle themselves in the neighbourhood of the towns, whilst the fortifications of Memphis itself had been suffered to fall into neglect. The Libyan people apparently regarded these settlements as a sort of advanced posts, and in the fifth year of Menephtah they were followed up by the further advance upon Egypt of an immense host, composed of the Libyans, their mercenary troops, and allies drawn from every part of North Africa, and possibly from more distant regions still. Tidings were brought the king that Marmaiu, the Libyan king, had 'sought out the best of all the combatants and of all the quick runners, and had brought his wife and children with him'—being apparently sure of success, and intent on finding a new home in the rich Egyptian land. No little alarm was excited throughout the country and even in the army itself, for we are told that the king addressed his troops 'with flashing eyes,' and upbraided them with trembling like geese, and not knowing what to do or how to meet the enemy. 'The pillagers,' he said, 'are devastating the country; they have come, following their chief, that they may gain cultivated lands, and fill their mouths with food daily. Fain would they establish themselves in Khemi. . . . Behold, I am your shepherd. Who is like me to keep life in his children? Should they be anxious and frightened like birds?' These remonstrances were received in silence. Then the king proceeded to declare that he would not 'await the enemy's approach, so that the land should be wasted by the advance of the foreign peoples. Their king is like a dog; he brags with his mouth, but his courage is naught.' Pharaoh's own heart, however, may not have been quite at ease, in spite of his brave speeches, when he retired to rest that night—but his confidence was revived by a dream. The god Ptah appeared to him, and put a scimitar into his hand, exhorting him to 'put away dejection and desponding thoughts.' 'What am I to do?' inquired the king. Ptah, in reply, directed him to proceed with all his forces, and join battle with the foe at Pi-ari-sheps (Prosopis). Accordingly, he there attacked the confederates, and gained a complete victory. The brunt of the battle, however, seems to have been borne by the mercenary troops. 'For six hours,' says the narrative, 'the foreign mercenaries of his majesty hewed down the foe. The sword gave no mercy, and the land was full of corpses.' The fugitives, amongst whom was the Libyan king himself, were pursued by the horsemen. All the goods and ornaments of the hostile prince were captured, and the skin tents of the Libyans burnt upon the field of battle. More than 14,000 were reckoned amongst the slain, and over 9000 were made prisoners. The battle of Prosopis secured tranquillity upon the frontier for a considerable time.

The reign of Seti Menephtah II. affords very little worthy of notice. It was quiet and uneventful, but was followed by a period of confusion and civil war. The names of rival kings are preserved, but the details of the history are very obscure. A good general impression, however, of the disastrous scenes amidst which the nineteenth dynasty closed is given by Rameses III., first king of the succeeding dynasty. 'The land,' he tells us, 'had fallen into confusion; each man did as he chose; there was no sovereign master. The princes of the nomes bore sway, and men slaughtered each other through fear and jealousy. The end of these years of calamity was that Aarsu, a Syrian by birth, gained the chief supremacy, and the whole land did him homage. The gods fared no better than men; their images were overthrown, and no oblations were brought to the temples.

'Then was Setnekht, the beloved of Amen, raised up by the gods. He was like Set in the day of his wrath, and terrible like the god of war. He took command of the whole country, and destroyed the evil-doers who had wasted Lower Egypt; he purified the great throne of Khemi, and restored that which had been disturbed. Each man saw and knew his brother again, from whom he had been separated as by a wall. The sacrifices were reinstated for the gods. He made me heir of the throne of Seb, and ruler of the lands of Khemi. Then he sought repose among the gods; the royal bark crossed the river, and he entered his eternal dwelling-place in Western Thebes.'

CHAPTER XII.

Twentieth and Twenty-first Dynasties—The Ramessidæ and the Priest-Kings. (*Circa* 1200-970 B.C.)

IT may be doubtful whether Rameses III., son of the Setnekht who pacified Egypt and restored order, was connected by blood with the preceding dynasties. He bore the name of an illustrious predecessor, however, and throughout his reign he appears to have made it his aim to emulate the great Rameses. His first task was to reorganise the public service, which had fallen into great disorder; to appoint and to regulate the station and office of the prince-governors, of the soldiers of the army and their foreign auxiliaries, of the inferior servants and the bondsmen. The earliest years of his reign were disturbed by invasion both from east and west. The Shashu and the Libyans, ever hanging on the confines, were always ready to cross the border of the Delta when opportunity served, and during the tumults, amidst which the nineteenth dynasty closed, such an opportunity certainly presented itself. After assailing the invaders and driving them back, Rameses transplanted his prisoners into large fortified places, where they were kept under guard, and a certain quantity of woven stuff and corn was yearly exacted from them, for the service of the temples. But a more dangerous foe remained to be assailed. A certain tribe, known as the Mashausha, had penetrated the land south of Memphis, had entered the oasis of the Fayoum, and had not only gradually crept south, but had advanced eastwards from the Fayoum to the Nile itself. Of certain towns these foreigners had even held possession for years. In the fifth year of his reign, Rameses III. attacked the Mashausha, and, after a fearful slaughter, drove them out of the land. The prisoners appear to have been employed as mercenaries in the army and navy, whilst their wives and children were removed to fortified places, and their flocks and herds confiscated to the service of the temple of Amen-Ra.

At the head of the Red Sea the king constructed a well, carefully guarded by fortifications, and reopened trade with Punt by way of Koptos and the sea. He also renewed the working of the *mafek*[1] and copper mines. Then he tells us he planted trees and shrubs throughout the land, that the people might sit under the shade, and he says further, that the country was so safe that the weakest woman might travel alone without fear of molestation. 'The soldiers of the horse and foot,' continues his account, 'live at ease; the Sardinian and Libyan auxiliaries stretch themselves full length upon their backs. They are not on the watch, for the enemy have ceased to invade. Their bows and arrows lie useless. They eat and drink with their wives and children, and make themselves merry. I am among them as a protector ready to defend.'

But soon another dark cloud, gathering in the distance, rapidly approached, and broke in a torrent of invasion upon the northern shore. The foe came this time from the distant regions of Asia Minor.

---

[1] Sometimes supposed to have been the turquoise, but it is doubtful whether correctly so.

The old claims of Egypt to supremacy in Asia had long been suffered to lapse, and the course of time brought many changes.

In the earliest ages, strong and civilised kingdoms (perhaps coeval with the pyramids) had existed at Ur, Larsa, and other cities of Chaldea. But they had fallen and passed away when Thothmes III. entered Mesopotamia. The country was then divided into petty principalities, which were subdued with little difficulty. By the time Rameses II. was on the throne (the fourteenth century B.C.), Nineveh and Babylon had become the capitals of strong and important states, and were constantly engaged in mortal conflict for supremacy. They were absorbed in this mutual strife and in warding off the hostile assaults of the Elamites and other neighbouring nations; neither state was as yet thinking of far-extended conquest and dominion. The Israelites entered Canaan and carried on a war of extermination against its inhabitants, but they only succeeded in establishing themselves in parts of the country, generally in the more hilly districts, as the Canaanites, possessing chariots and horses, were able to maintain possession of the plains. The Egyptians probably viewed this fierce conflict with indifference, careful only that the great military road should not be interfered with, and the Israelites, maintaining their hold of the 'promised land' with much difficulty, were by no means prepared for any such attempt. North of Syria the power of the Kheta had greatly diminished, and was still further weakened by the assault of a mighty host of confederated tribes, which, emerging at this juncture from the hills and coast lands of Asia Minor, poured in a resistless stream towards the south. With them may have been allied, in hope of plunder, Etruscans, pirates from of old, and not unlikely roving Greeks from the isles and shores of the Mediterranean, probably little better than pirates themselves. For this formidable onslaught was made by sea and land simultaneously. The land forces defeated the Kheta, occupied Kadi (Galilee), and pitched their camp for a while in the land of the Amorites, ravaging and plundering as they went. The sequel may be described in the graphic narrative of Rameses III.: 'They came leaping from their coasts and islands, and spread themselves at once over all lands; no people stood before their arms. Their nostrils snuffed the air of the southern lands; their desire was to breathe a balmy atmosphere. On they came against the Egyptian land. But there was in readiness a fiery furnace before their faces on the side of Egypt. Their hearts were full of confidence, their minds of plans. But an ambush was prepared for them, and they were taken in the snare like birds. They who reached the boundaries of my land never reaped harvest more. Their soul and spirit passed away for ever. A mighty firebrand was lighted before those who were assembled on the great sea in front of the mouths of the river. A wall of iron shut them in on the lake. They were caught like birds in a net, and were made prisoners; their ships and all they possessed lay strewn on the mirror of the water. Those who came by the way of the land, Amen-Ra pursued and annihilated them. Thus have I taken from the nations the desire to direct their thoughts against Egypt.' This account of the great battle of Migdol, which secured a long period of repose from hostile attack, is inscribed upon the walls of the great temple which Rameses III. erected not far from the colossi of Amenhotep III. in Western Thebes. Here are also pictorial representations of the scene where naval warfare is for the first time depicted. No doubt the services of the mercenaries, so largely employed in the fleet, stood the Egyptians in good stead at this crisis, the naval service never being popular with the native population.

The great temple of Rameses III. at Medinet Habou (to which, for the first time, so far as we know, a palace was annexed) was enriched with vast donations by the king; he also conferred immense gifts on other temples, which are detailed in almost endless lists. For Rameses III., at some period, undertook wars of retribution, and won victories, and acquired rich spoil, both on the mainland and in the Mediterranean isles, more especially in Cilicia and in Cyprus. Fabulous stories were current in after times concerning King Rampsinitus (as the Greeks called this monarch) and his wonderful treasure-house. Herodotus heard some of these sensational narratives, and recorded them at full length in his writings.

In the construction of this temple, Rameses III. did not scruple to employ materials taken from those of his predecessors. Bricks with the names of Seti I. and Rameses II. were freely used to build up its walls. Nor was this all he borrowed, for, as if he had not acquired sufficient renown on his own account, he adopted an inscription in honour of Rameses the Great as his own. It is a long panegyric in the most grandiloquent language, and not only abounds in general phrases of much high-flown glorification of the king, but especially commemorates his building up of the city of Zoan and his first meeting with the Princess of Kheta. Rameses III. had the whole panegyric copied, with a few slight necessary changes. He, however, let it appear as if he had been the builder of Zoan, only stopping short of claiming the Khetan princess as his bride. It is curious that, after all, these attempts of the third Rameses to associate and almost to identify himself with the second Rameses may be said to have so far succeeded that they were in fact often confused with each other by foreign historians, and it is doubtful to this day which of the two was meant by the Sesostris of the Greeks—the probability being that he was a personage created out the confused traditions of both the Egyptian conquerors.

In spite of riches and renown, the throne of the third Rameses was not too securely based. It may have been that he was not of the ancient race, so long venerated and deified by the people, or it may have been that there was a general decay in Egyptian loyalty, but the fact is certain that a conspiracy of the most alarming extent was discovered, originating in the royal household itself. The conspirators were detected in time, and the record of their trial has been preserved. Many officers of high rank and many ladies in the palace were implicated. The first page of the papyrus is unfortunately defaced, so that the precise object and nature of the plot must remain uncertain. The royal commission to the judges is in the following terms :—' Those who are accused by the country I give them into your charge. As to the talk of men I know nothing about it.

Go ye and judge. Let what they have done be upon their own heads.' Sentence of death[1] was pronounced on most of the criminals, others were condemned to have their noses and ears cut off, the women appear to have been sentenced to a sort of penal servitude.

Amongst the means resorted to by the conspirators magic and sorcery played a conspicuous part. One Penhi, superintendent of the herds, is reported to have said :—' If only I possessed a writing that would give me power and strength!' Having succeeded in procuring such a writing, an 'enchantment fell upon him so that he gained admittance to the women's house and to the deep and secret place. He made human figures in wax for the purpose of alienating the mind of one of the maidens and of bewitching another, inciting them to all kinds of wickedness and villainy by his writings.'

There is good evidence that the practice of sorcery and magical arts of all sorts was greatly on the increase. The very tales that have been preserved belonging to this period are of won-

[1] The wording of the judgment seems to imply a judicial suicide.

der and enchantment; superstition was rife on all hands. The god especially honoured under the twentieth dynasty was the oracle-giving Khons;[1] the chapters of the ritual assigned to this date are full of elaborate ceremonial, and the use of certain portions as a spell or talisman is more and more insisted on. Great virtue was also assigned to the mere repetition of long and apparently meaningless names. Omens of all kinds were much regarded, and so were lucky and unlucky days in the calendar.[2] Nevertheless, alongside of these superstitious notions and practices there existed a higher and a nobler life; no hymns preserved to us are more lofty and beautiful in tone than some that are assigned to this period. In one addressed to Amen-Ra, we read :—

'O Ra, adored in Thebes! Thy love pervades the earth. Thou makest grass for the cattle and fruit-bearing trees for men. He causeth fish to live in the river, and giveth food to the birds upon the wing,

---

[1] Khons was the son of Amen and of Mut, the 'divine mother,' and formed with them the sacred triad of Thebes: but his worship never assumed a prominent place before this period. In many respects resembling Thoth, and, like him, connected with the moon, he was the especial god of the priesthood and giver of oracles.

[2] Tiele, *Hist. of Egyp. Relig.*

food to the mice in their holes, and to the flying creatures on the trees.

'Hail to thee! say all creatures, from the height of heaven to the breadth of the earth, and to the deep places of the sea—Adoration unto thee who hast created us!

'The spirits thou hast made bow down before thee; the gods adore thy majesty. We, the creatures of thy hand, praise thee for our being, we give thanks to thee for thy mercy towards us,—whose name is hidden from his creatures—in his Name which is AMEN.'[1]

The hymn to the Nile, which is ascribed to the preceding dynasty, is very remarkable from the twofold aspect it presents us. At first we seem to behold only the river or some local deity impersonated in the river:—

> 'Hail to thee, O Nile!
> Coming in peace, giving life to Khemi,
> Watering the land unceasingly,
> He maketh the fields ready for the plough;
> Every creature receiveth food.'

After the song has proceeded for some time in this strain, all on a sudden the Nile disappears from view, and the worshipper is in the presence of the divine and unutterable, though with no apparent change of person:—

[1] The Hidden or Unseen.

> ' He is not graven in marble,
> No eye of man can behold him;
> He hath no ministers nor offerings!
> He is not adored in sanctuaries,
> His dwelling is not known;
> No shrine is found, nor pictured words,
> No building may contain him!'

But then the loftier strain subsides again, and the hymn closes with the words:—

> Shine forth, shine forth, O Nile!
> Giving life to men by his oxen,
> Life to his oxen by his meadow land—
> Shine forth, shine forth, O Nile!'

Rameses III. constructed for himself in the 'valley of the kings,' a tomb which contained eight or ten chambers adorned with pictures of scenes taken from both the present and the future life. Amongst them occurs one evidently intended as an allegoric representation of the hope of life after death—' The horizon of heaven supported by a female figure, and the sun just rising above it; this is so placed that a ray of light can penetrate from the entrance of the tomb, 350 feet off, and pass over the sarcophagus and illuminate this emblem of eternal hope.'[1]

The thirteen succeeding sovereigns all bore

[1] Villiers Stuart, *Nile Gleanings*.

the name of Rameses, but hardly any record is left of their reigns. There are inscriptions extant which belong to this period, lofty and bombastic in the extreme, and exceeding in the pompous assumption of their style those of their predecessors, if possible. They are mere empty phrases, which produce only an impression of absurdity when applied to the Ramessidæ as they pass across the stage in monotonous succession, and leave behind no achievements or triumphs either of peace or of war. The fourth, sixth, and seventh of these kings were sons of Rameses III.; the fifth of the name was a usurper, so it is not likely that the reigns of all the four together occupied any considerable period. One or two of the Ramessidæ constructed tombs for themselves in the 'valley of the kings;' they were given to carving their names and inscriptions on the monuments of their predecessors, but all of them in succession did not quite achieve the completion of the small oracle-temple of Khons, which was the family sanctuary of their house. The chief event which is recorded of these dull times is, however, significant, as showing how the profound sense of veneration for the 'eternal dwelling-places' of the departed must have been deadened, if not lost. In the reign of Rameses IX., it was discovered that there was an organised scheme for breaking open and plundering the tombs supposed most likely to contain treasure; the resting-places of the sovereigns themselves were not respected. The accused were brought to trial, and a careful investigation of the tombs was instituted. It was found that in many cases the difficult task of reaching the carefully concealed sarcophagus had been successfully accomplished; the mummies had been dragged out, and the funeral gifts, and aught else of value, carried off. Under the twentieth dynasty the throne was no longer safe from conspiracy and domestic treason; the very sanctity of the grave was violated, and the mummies of the departed were not secure from outrage and plunder.

The oracle-temple of Khons was consulted on every important occasion, and its fame seems to have spread far beyond the limits of Egypt itself. A curious episode belonging to the reign of Rameses XII. has been preserved, in a story written on the walls of this temple. It relates that the king had married a princess of the land of Bakhten, and that on a certain festival day there came a messenger from that country bringing presents for the king, accompanied by a request from the King of Bakhten. His daughter, the younger sister of the Queen of Egypt, had become possessed by a strange malady, and his majesty implored that a learned man acquainted with such things might be sent from Egypt to see her. Rameses XII. accordingly sent a learned man thither, who found the princess 'in the state of one possessed with spirits,' but the spirit was hostile, nor could the learned man prevail over him. A second message came from the troubled father, entreating that an Egyptian god might be sent to Bakhten. Pharaoh was standing before the shrine of the oracle-giving Khons, who was especially noted for power over such maladies. On inquiring whether the god would be willing to undertake the journey, the king received a favourable answer. Accordingly the shrine of Khons was borne upon the shoulders of twelve priests the whole way from

Egypt to Bakhten, a journey of one year and five months, attended by chariots and horsemen on the right hand and on the left. The king and the princes came forth to meet and to welcome the ark, and prostrated themselves on the ground before it, and the god proceeded to the palace where the princess was, and speedily effected a cure. The expelled spirit thereupon made a humble submission to the god as his slave, and expressed his readiness to return whence he came—only, he asked that, first of all, a great sacrifice might be made in his honour. His request was granted, and, says the story, 'the spirit went in peace wherever he chose by order of Khons, the giver of oracles. The prince of the land of Bakhten was very much delighted, and so was every one in the land. He said: "I will not let this god go back to Egypt; he shall stay in my country." Three years, four months, five weeks, and one day did the god remain in Bakhten. Then it happened that the king saw in a dream the god come out of his shrine in the likeness of a hawk of gold; he spread forth his wings and flew on high towards the land of

Khemi. When the king awoke he was troubled in his mind, and he called the prophet of Khons and said to him : " This god is hostile to us, let us send him back to Egypt." And he gave him many presents, besides troops and very many horsemen. They reached Egypt in peace, and the presents were offered to the god. So Khons re-entered his house in peace in the thirty-third year of the king's reign.'

The custom now so prevalent of consulting the oracle, and of acting according to its dictates, is one amongst other significant signs of the increasing power and influence of the priesthood and of the part they were gradually assuming in the government of the country. Under Rameses IX. the positions of king and priest seem already reversed. In former days the kings recorded the story of the magnificent buildings they erected in honour of the gods, and the munificent gifts with which they endowed the temples, received by the priesthood with loyal gratitude. But in the reign of Rameses IX. it is a chief priest of Amen-Ra who carves upon the temple wall a full account of all *he* has done in rebuilding and adorning the sacred edifice—the 'holy house of the chief priests of Amen.' He, however, inscribes upon the work the full name of Pharaoh, and thus dedicates it to the king, who duly acknowledges his obligation, and orders rich rewards and honours to be bestowed upon the chief priest in token of the royal gratitude.

The shadowy forms of the Ramessid kings grow more and more indistinct; of the three last, whose names are preserved as the fourteenth, fifteenth, and sixteenth Rameses, it is quite uncertain whether they were ever crowned in Thebes. The power of the chief priests during the reign of so many feeble monarchs had, on the other hand, steadily increased, until the government of the country was virtually in their hands. Their ambition grew with what it fed on, and by repeated intermarriages with princesses of the royal house, they might seem to acquire a certain legitimate claim to the throne, of which they at last took possession—Her-hor, 'chief priest and first prophet of Amen,' being proclaimed King of Upper and Lower Egypt probably about 1100 B.C.

The priests of Egypt formed, as we know,

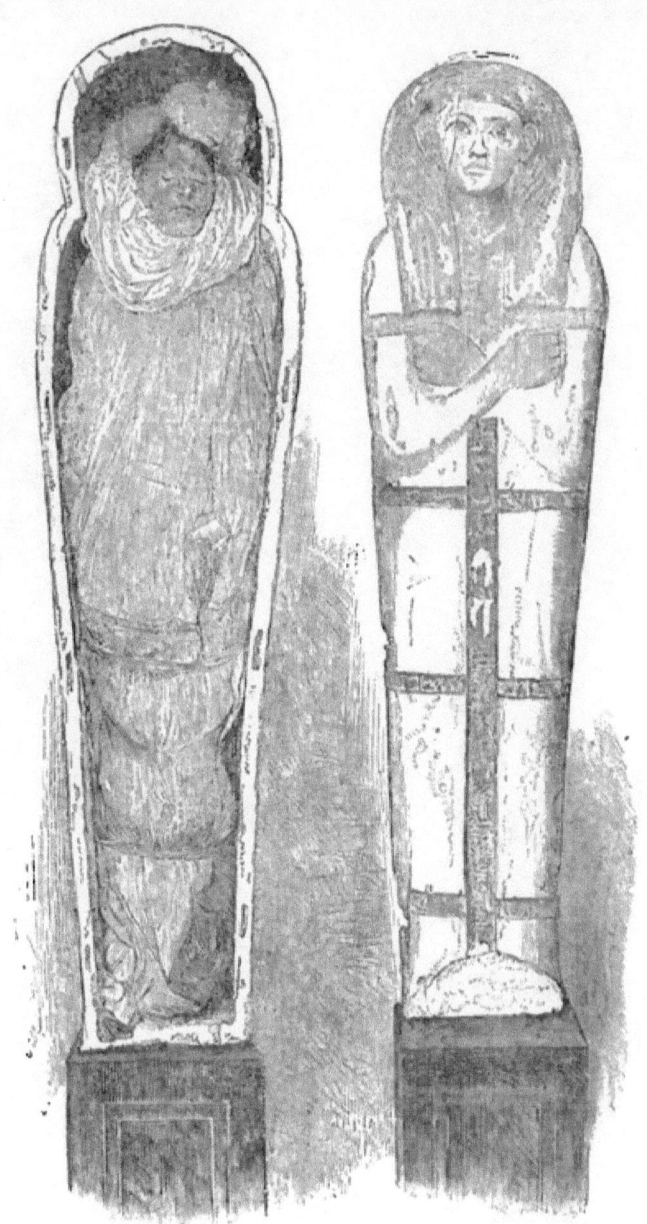

Mummy and Mummy-case of the Priest Nebseni.

no distinct and isolated caste. They were governors of cities, commanders on the battle-field, physicians, architects, scribes; and thus were often seen in secular employments, although they alone could enter within the sacred recesses of the temple and officiate in its services. The kings themselves were so far regarded as priests, that they were admitted to perform sacred rites, and thus the regal and sacerdotal offices had long been in some sense blended before Her-hor assumed the crown as the first sovereign of the twenty-first dynasty—the dynasty of the priest-kings.

The sovereigns of this dynasty showed an especial solicitude in preserving from injury and outrage the mortal remains of their predecessors. They continued the custom, which had prevailed since the spoliation of tombs came to light under Rameses IX., of a periodical inspection, carried out officially, the results of which were recorded on the spot by a scribe. Her-hor chose for his own family burial-place a lonely spot not far from the terraced temple of Queen Hatasu. A mass of broken rock almost hid the entrance, whence, by the descent of a perpendicular shaft, 25 feet deep, by 7 feet wide, a subterranean gallery of 200 feet in length was reached. Beyond was the vault, which measured about 25 feet by 14. There were either six or seven sovereigns of the twenty-first dynasty; and the last but one of them foreseeing, it is not unlikely, that a time of trouble and danger was at hand, gathered into the gloomy unadorned recesses of the gallery and vault of his family tomb the coffins of many illustrious predecessors. He then appears to have finally closed the tomb and suffered himself to be buried elsewhere. It was here that the remains of so many Egyptian sovereigns, both of the twenty-first and of earlier dynasties, were found in the great discovery of 1881. The little we know concerning even the names and succession of the priestly dynasty has been chiefly derived from this their family burial-place. We find that four of them married wives who were princesses in their own right. One of these queens, wife of Pinotem II., fourth king of the dynasty, is buried with her new-born babe by her side. The papyrus, containing portions of the ritual, which according to custom was laid in the sarcophagus, is in perfect preservation; it is beautifully written, and is full of richly-coloured illustrations, of which the tints are as fresh as if laid on yesterday. The last sovereign buried in this tomb was the wife of the king who finally closed it. With her were found

Mummy of a Gazelle.

the usual funereal papyrus, vases, and small statues; and besides these there was the rich and beautifully adorned canopy under which her body had been conveyed across the river to the city of the dead, and in a hamper by her side was the funeral repast of meat and fruits, which, being dedicated to her, show her to have been the last occupant of the family vault. With the mummy of the deceased queen was interred a mummied gazelle, that had probably been a pet with her in her lifetime. Both vault and gallery were now full, and the king closed it; his own tomb and that of his successor, the last monarch of the dynasty, are unknown.

CHAPTER XIII.

Shishak I. and the Twenty-second (Bubastite) Dynasty—The Ethiopian Kings—The Assyrians in Egypt—Sack of Thebes. (*Circa* 970–666 B.C.)

IT might seem as though the name of Rameses had power sufficient to hold together the fabric of the state so long as the twentieth dynasty was on the throne. With the dethronement and exile of the Ramessid kings, all unity was at an end. Her-hor had claimed the sovereignty of all Egypt, but his successors ruled over a diminishing territory, and the dominion of the last of the priest-kings did not probably extend much, if at all, beyond the Thebaid. Whilst they had been reigning at Thebes, an independent dynasty (regarded indeed by Manetho as the twenty-first), ruled in the Delta, having its seat at Tanis, *i.e.* Zoan. But the Delta had long been the home of naturalised foreigners of different nationalities, and amongst them were settlers bearing Assyrian names—warlike and ambitious men, apparently of distinguished birth, who intermarried with princesses of the Ramessid family, and succeeded in founding the twenty-second dynasty. The names of the family who thus came to the front are clearly not Egyptian,—Nimruth, Usarkon, Takelath are the Assyrian Nimrod, Sargon, and Tiglath; but whilst their names point to an Assyrian origin, their religion and customs had become purely Egyptian, even before they set up their throne at Bubastis.[1] The first sovereign of this dynasty was Sheshenk (the Shishak of the Old Testament), who gained the ascendency over the whole land, and drove the last of the priest-kings to take refuge in Nubia. The city of Napata, standing on the bank of the Nile, and near a lofty hill known as the Holy Mountain, became the seat of the sacerdotal kings. It was a fertile, prosperous, and peaceful region, and

[1] The Egyptian Pa-Bast, or the city of Bast. It was situated in the eastern portion of the Delta, and was of immemorial antiquity. Under the kings of the twenty-second dynasty, it attained great splendour, and the worship of Bast became wide-spread and popular. Herodotus saw her magnificent temple, and the festival celebrated in her honour with such splendour and revelry. Bast was almost identical with Sechet—the lioness and the cat were sacred to her. Her worship was exceedingly popular under the later dynasties, and this led to the widespread reverence with which the cat was regarded in those days.

its people, long ago completely Egyptianised, were devoted to the worship of Amen-Ra. Here the priest-kings disappeared from sight, but not for ever.

It has been conjectured that the founders of the twenty-second or Bubastite dynasty may have been fugitives of high birth from Assyria, who had been hospitably received and honourably entertained in Egypt. The fortunes of Assyria were indeed at this time at a very low ebb, after having risen very high. The long-continued struggle between Assyria and Babylon already alluded to (p. 215) had ended in the complete ascendency of the former state. About the middle of the twelfth century, the first Assyrian empire rose, and lasted for about seventy years. It was an empire based on mere military ascendency, was maintained by force and cruelty, and rested on no enduring foundation. The Kings of Assyria subdued Babylon, and conquered the Hittites (the Kheta of Rameses II.) and other neighbouring nations. But in process of time the Hittites rose in arms, and were joined by the Babylonians (ever restless under the Assyrian supremacy), and the

Assyrian empire fell before their combined attack. For some time, it would seem, there was not even an independent sovereign reigning at Nineveh.

The time was propitious for the growth and development of new states. Assyria was prostrate, Babylon unaggressive, Egypt inert, the Hittites content with their newly recovered independence.

The cities of Phœnicia, on the coast of Palestine, were engaged, as of old, in busy commerce throughout the known world, coming even so far as to the British Isles in quest of tin. They colonised, but did not conquer other lands. Their religion, with its cruel and licentious rites, was the same as that of the neighbouring Canaanitish tribes, but the latter were probably greatly inferior in civilisation; they still maintained their ground in certain parts of Palestine.

During the times of the Judges there had been no national unity amongst the Israelites—no central controlling power; they were still in the tribal state. The Philistines, a small but strong and warlike nationality, settled in the southern towns of the sea-coast, almost expelled them from the land. Disarmed and helpless, they were furtively hiding in the caves of the limestone hills, when, under the energetic leadership of Saul, they arose to repel the foe. The Philistines were defeated, but the strife continued, and in the end the monarchy of Saul was overthrown. It was reserved for David to subdue these inveterate foes, to capture Jerusalem from the Canaanites, and make it the centre of a kingdom which he enlarged by continual wars with the neighbouring states, until he bequeathed to Solomon an Israelitish empire—peaceful, wealthy, and magnificent whilst it lasted, but destined scarcely to outlast the generation that had seen its foundation. Between the sovereign of this new empire and the ancient monarchy of Egypt there was close friendship and alliance, and a 'daughter of Pharaoh'[1] became Queen of Israel. Close commercial intercourse was also kept up. Hitherto, the Israelites had been content to employ asses and mules, and

[1] Probably a princess of the dynasty ruling at Tanis; the priest-kings, whose seat of power was in the far south, are less likely to have connected themselves with the kingdom of Israel.

their troops had consisted of infantry only, but Solomon introduced horses and chariots in great numbers from the land of Egypt, both for domestic use and for military service. It may be possible to trace Egyptian influence in the Israelitish court. It may have kindled the love of Solomon for natural history, or have suggested his first expedition to the land of spices; it may have moulded certain parts of the architecture of temple and of palace, or have left its traces on the literature of the time. All this is possible, though little more than guesswork. Nor did the alliance last long; it was sundered even before luxury and despotism had undermined and overthrown the empire of Solomon. Sheshenk I., the founder of the twenty-second dynasty, was on the Egyptian throne when the fugitive Jeroboam arrived in Egypt—his heart full of his ambitious schemes, and on the death of Solomon it was not with his son, but with his rebellious servant Jeroboam that the Egyptian monarchy was in alliance. Shishak marched into Judah, entered Jerusalem, and carried off thence the treasures both of the temple and palace of King Solomon. The

Levites, throughout the land, had remained faithful to the house of David and the service of the temple, and Shishak, it appears, captured and despoiled many of their cities, even those that lay in the kingdom of Israel. The names of all the towns subdued by him in this campaign are recorded on the walls of the temple at Karnak.

The hostility of the Levites to the rule of Jeroboam is easy to understand, as he set up a rival worship of his own at Dan and Bethel, and appointed priests of his own selection. The form assumed by the objects of this worship might very possibly have been adopted by Jeroboam in remembrance of what he had seen in Egypt, and even as a pledge of his alliance with its king. Never, indeed, had the worship of Apis reached so extravagant a pitch as under this dynasty. In the Serapeum, the burial-place of the sacred bulls, are still preserved the tablets which tell of their installation, death, and interment. 'On such a day of the month and year,' say the records, 'this great god was carried to his rest in the beautiful region of the west—at rest with the great gods —with Osiris, and with the gods and goddesses of the west. His glory was sought for in all places of Pi-tomih (Lower Egypt). He was found after some months in the city of Ha-shed-abtu, after they had searched through all the lakes and islands. He was solemnly introduced into the temple of Ptah, beside his father Ptah.' The date is carefully given, and the full lifetime of the 'god.' The burial of the Apis was on a scale of regal magnificence, and a national mourning of seventy days was observed. The finding of a successor[1] and his installation was celebrated with the wildest exultation, and with national rejoicing. Little room is left for the idea of symbol or sign; the sacred creature is an emanation of the Divine, is a 'god,' and as such the object of the grossest and most grotesque idolatry. An indescribable national enthusiasm gathered around the Apis —he was lodged with sumptuous magnificence, the centre of a crowd of devotees and of those who came to learn the secrets of the future.[2]

---

[1] The Apis must be black, with certain white marks of mystical import.

[2] One mode of consulting the sacred bull was by offering him food. Germanicus is said to have thus consulted him; the Apis refused to eat, and this unfavourable reception was considered to have foreboded his untimely fate.

THE WORSHIP OF APIS. FROM A STATUETTE IN THE BRITISH MUSEUM.

The successive deaths and interments of the Apis bulls, form, in fact, very nearly all the events recorded during the reigns of the eight kings who succeeded the warlike Shishak. Takelath II., the sixth in succession of this dynasty, sent his son Usarkon, who had been appointed high priest of Amen, to Thebes, to examine and to regulate the temple endowments there. The same inscription tells of some celestial portent which excited general attention, and was considered to portend trouble at hand.

Celestial omens were hardly needed to tell that dark days were near. The last kings of the twenty-second dynasty had to contend with rival princes who founded dynasties in the Delta, and, in the hopeless confusion arising from the mutual jealousies and struggles for supremacy amongst these contending families, the descendants of the priest-kings, closely watching the course of events from their Nubian retreat,[1] beheld the long looked-for opportunity arrived. About the middle of the eighth

---

[1] The country known as Nubia then formed part of the land of Kush, *i.e.* Ethiopia.

century B.C., they had already established their dominion at Thebes, where they had been warmly welcomed, and they were putting forth claims to a supremacy over the whole land. One of the warring princes in the north, Tafnekht, ruler of Sais, had at the same time formed a scheme for reducing the country to his allegiance. He was commander of the mercenary troops, who, in such unsettled times, might well avail to turn the balance in favour of any warlike and ambitious leader. Of the conflict that ensued we possess a full and interesting account, recorded in an inscription at Napata by Piankhi-meramen, the ruler of the south. Disquieting intelligence reached the king in his Nubian stronghold. Tafnekht 'was advancing up the river; multitudes of soldiers followed him, and the chiefs and governors were like dogs at his feet. No fortress was closed to him; the cities had opened their gates at his approach.' Thebes was in consternation, and appealed to Piankhi against the invader: 'Art thou silent and forgetful of the southern land as well as of the middle country?'

Piankhi despatched troops without delay; at

their setting forth the priest-king solemnly enjoined them to perform all due ceremonial rites and purifications on entering the city of Thebes. 'Lay down your arms before the Divine Leader; there is no victory gained over men without his knowledge. Glorious deeds hath he wrought by his mighty arm; many shall be turned back by a few, one man shall put a thousand to flight. Prostrate yourselves before him, and say: "Cover for us the path of war with the shadow of thy scimitar, grant strength unto the young men whom thou hast appointed, that they may cast down many ten thousands."' The army of Piankhi encountered the enemy, and defeated them. King Nimrod,[1] ruler of Hermopolis, one of the confederated princes, hearing of their victorious advance, hastened to shut himself up in his city, and prepared to stand a siege. Piankhi's troops continued to be successful in repeated encounters with the foe, but their king was not content, for Hermopolis was untaken. Priests had been accustomed to appear on the battle-field from

---

[1] A descendant, doubtless, of the twenty-second dynasty kings, of Assyrian origin.

the days of old, so that there was nothing anomalous in Piankhi's now girding on the sword and appearing in person on the scene. 'Behold, they have made a stand!' he cried reproachfully to his forces; 'you have fought them without courage; will you not complete the pursuit, spreading the fear of my name even unto the north of the land of Egypt?'

Animated by the presence of the king, the troops now pressed the siege with redoubled energy, and the town surrendered 'prostrate in supplication before the face of the sovereign.' Nimrod first sent his wife and the princesses to intercede with the conqueror, and afterwards offered his own humble submission with many gifts, which Piankhi graciously accepted. He entered Hermopolis, and, on examining the state of things in general, was roused to anger by discovering that certain horses there had been left without sufficient food. He expressed the bitterest displeasure,—'Vile are they to my heart that have starved my horses; more is this than any other abomination that thou, O Nimrod, hast wrought altogether!'

After this decisive victory, other princes and

governors came in and offered their submission; and various towns surrendered to the promised clemency of the conqueror. Mertum, indeed, had closed its gates; but 'his majesty sent to them, saying, "Two ways are before you; choose as you will—open and live; shut the gates and die. His majesty does not pass by any closed fort." And lo! they opened forthwith.'

Meantime Tafnekht had thrown himself into Memphis with 8000 men, both soldiers and marines; he had provisioned it carefully and strengthened the fortifications. King Piankhi, says the story, 'found the lofty walls strengthened with new works, and the bulwarks fitted up with great strength. There was no way found to assault it.' But Tafnekht himself slipped away as soon as the siege began; his troops (probably the mercenaries), deprived of the encouragement of their leader's presence, were disheartened, and Memphis yielded to a combined assault by land and water. 'The city was taken as by a storm of rain; multitudes were slain within it, or brought as captives to his majesty.' Next day, Piankhi entered, as was his custom in every captured town, the temples; there he offered sacrifices to Ptah and to the other gods.

Piankhi afterwards visited the ancient and far-famed City of the Sun, not far from Memphis. There he 'offered oblations on the waters of the lake of Horus; he purified himself in the heart of the cool lake, bathing his face in the stream of the sacred waters, wherein Ra bathes his countenance daily.' Then on the sandy heights of On he made 'a great sacrifice before the face of Ra at his rising.' The priest-king then demanded admission into the innermost sanctuary and to the sacred shrine of the god.

The chief priest, possibly somewhat dismayed, offered intercession for the king, duly purified him with incense and sprinkling, and brought him garlands from the temple of the obelisks. He girded on the sacred vestments, and, passing through the outer halls, advanced within the most holy place. 'The king stood himself, the great one alone; he drew the bolt, he threw back the doors, he saw the face of his father Ra in the temple, and on the sacred bark. Then he closed the doors, and set thereon seals of clay marked with the royal signet, and he commanded the priests, saying : " I have set my seal ; let no other king whatever enter therein." [1]

During his stay at Memphis the king received the submission and the tributary offerings of all the petty governors and kings, but of those who sought to enter the royal presence none were admitted but Nimrod, because 'he was not an eater of fish,[2] a thing forbidden in the royal palace.'

Tafnekht did not appear in person from his distant retreat; he sent his submission by an embassy—' Hail to thee! I could not look upon thy face nor stand before thy terror. I have reached the islands of the Mediterranean. Behold! thy servant is cleansed from his pride. I beseech thee to take my goods into thy treasury, the gold and all the precious stones. O send a messenger unto me as a reconciler.' Piankhi, after having received the submission of the confederated opponents, returned to Thebes with great rejoicing and triumph.

It is very doubtful, however, whether the

[1] This would be meant to apply only to all the rival claimants to sovereignty in the north, not to his own successors.

[2] The priests were prohibited from eating fish, which was considered as unclean food—at any rate sea fish, of which the more devout and scrupulous Egyptians would not partake.

supremacy, thus triumphantly acquired, was maintained even so long as during Piankhi's own lifetime. His successor, Nut-meramen, was moved by a dream to reconquer it. 'His majesty beheld two snakes, one to his right, the other to his left, and when he awoke he found them no more. He said: "Explain these things to me in a moment," and lo! they explained it to him, saying: "Thou wilt have the southern lands, and thou shalt seize upon the northern, and both crowns shall be set upon thy head."'

The king, collecting a numerous army, advanced down the stream, and met with no opposition until he reached Memphis. Here he gained a victory, whereupon the 'chiefs of the north' entered their walled towns, so that there was no reaching their retreats. A pause ensued, neither party seeming willing to take further steps. However, the suspense ended by a voluntary surrender of the northern princes, who came to Memphis to offer their homage, and were gladly received and hospitably entertained. Being dismissed from the royal presence, they returned to their respective governments, and the 'men of the north' sailed up to the place where his majesty was, to offer gifts and tribute in token of fealty.

The power of the twenty-fifth or 'Ethiopian' dynasty was gradually increasing and consolidating itself; its supremacy was in the end recognised in some sort throughout the land, although in Lower Egypt it was always uncertain and precarious. The descendants of the 'chiefs of the north' never rendered more than a reluctant and sullen obedience to the rulers from the south. The successors of Piankhi, however, were not content to rule, as he had done, from their distant seat in Napata, but they set up their throne in the heart of Egypt itself, claiming and, as far as possible, exercising the rights of an over-lord.

Stormy times were close at hand, and a strong hand and a resolute will would be wanted at the helm. The Assyrian power, reviving from its deep depression, had gradually gained strength. Tiglath-Pileser II. (744-726 B.C.) was the founder of the second Assyrian empire, destined to be for more than a century the scourge of every neighbouring nation, and the dread of those that were far off. The lesser states that had risen to power on the fall of the first Assyrian empire, instead of friendly alliance against a common foe, continued the policy of mutual rivalry and bitter antagonism —thus preparing the way for the conqueror's feet. The two kingdoms into which the empire of Solomon had been split were at enmity with each other, and both were constantly at feud with the king of Syria. On the accession of the feeble Ahaz to the throne of Judah he was sore pressed by the assaults of the Edomites and Philistines, and panic-stricken by the news of a coalition formed by the kings of Syria and Israel to dethrone him and set up a creature of their own in his place. 'At that time did Ahaz send to the kings of Assyria to help him.' In an evil hour he declared himself the vassal of Tiglath-Pileser, and confiscated the treasures of the temple, as an offering to his new master. In swift response the Assyrian king advanced, took Damascus, carried its people away captive, and destroyed the power of Syria with a blow. With another fell swoop he desolated the Israelitish territory east of the Jordan, and carried into captivity the tribes who dwelt there. His successor, Shalmaneser, crossed the Jordan, and marching upon Samaria, reduced Hoshea, king of Israel, to vassalage. It was not long, however, before Hoshea threw off the Assyrian yoke, ceased to pay tribute, and sought the aid of Shebek (or Sabaco, the So of 2 Kings xvii. 4), who had succeeded Piankhi on the throne. But the forces sent by Shebek, or by some of the other princes of the north, were routed, and Hoshea carried prisoner to Assyria—' cut off like foam upon the water.' The siege of Samaria was begun, but Shalmaneser died soon after. It was his successor Sargon, who not only captured Ashdod, after defeating the Egypto-Ethiopian forces, who aided in its defence, but brought the siege of Samaria to a close 721 B.C., and carried the people of the land into captivity. Egypt, unable to afford any efficient help, seems to have become an asylum of some of the ' outcasts of Israel.'[1]

Ahaz of Judah appears to have continued submissive and tributary to the end of his days, but his son Hezekiah inaugurated a nobler

---

[1] Compare Isa. xi. 11, xxvii. 13; Hosea ix. 6.

policy. He cast off the Assyrian yoke, and sought the alliance of Taharak (Tirhakah), king of Ethiopia and Egypt. Tirhakah, at the early age of twenty, began his troubled and eventful reign. Many years had to be spent in assuring his own sovereignty over the land he claimed to rule. That land was, as he must have known, the prize on which the Assyrian kings had 'cast their eyes,' but, whilst his grasp of the central power was so uncertain, inaction and delay appeared the safest policy—'their strength was to sit still' (Isa. xxx. 7.) The Delta being always in a state of disaffection and disunion, it was no easy task to undertake military enterprises beyond the borders—'city' being ever ready to 'fight against city, and kingdom against kingdom' (see Isa. xix. 2).

Meantime the rush of Assyrian invasion had swept over Palestine. Sargon had attacked Ashdod; Sennacherib directed his march upon Lachish; both lay on the road that led to Egypt, towards which country the Assyrians had been gradually creeping nearer and nearer across the ruins of conquered states.

Forty-six fenced cities of Judah, besides many smaller towns, were taken and plundered by the invaders, and Hezekiah was 'shut up in Jerusalem like a bird in his cage.' The king of Judah delayed no longer to send his humble submission, and the arrears of his unpaid tribute, to Sennacherib encamped before Lachish. But the submission was hollow and the tribute extorted, for Hezekiah was in treaty with Egypt all the while. His messengers made the weary journey through the burning desert, their camels and asses laden with gifts and offerings,[1] to implore the aid of the king, who seems then to have been at Zoan in the Delta —preparing at last to march against the foe. Nor was the haughty Assyrian monarch unaware of the secret hopes of the king of Judah. He had captured Lachish, with the cruel massacre and torture of the captives that usually accompanied Assyrian conquests. His attack upon Libnah was postponed, for tidings came that Tirhakah, at the head of the Egypto-Ethiopian army, had crossed the frontiers. Aware of the secret understanding

---

[1] Isa. xxx. 4-7.

between that sovereign and the king of Judah, Sennacherib vented his bitter indignation and scorn in menaces and insult. He now demanded from Hezekiah nothing less than unconditional and absolute surrender, and taunted him with his vain reliance upon that 'broken reed,' the king of Egypt. At this crisis silence falls upon the scene, a silence broken only by the exulting cry of the great Hebrew prophet, as the mighty Assyrian host perishes before an unseen foe.

Judah breathed freely again, and a respite was accorded to Egypt, though not of long duration. Sennacherib, though engaged in many warlike enterprises during the remainder of his reign, left it to his successor Esar-haddon (680-668 B.C.), to renew the attempt upon Egypt. Judah was unmolested this time, and took no part in the terrible and desolating struggle that ensued.

Tirhakah had entered into an alliance with the king of Tyre, against the common foe. Esar-haddon laid siege to Tyre, and then, advancing along the old military road, trodden of old by the armies of Thothmes and of

Rameses in the opposite direction, he entered Egypt. Tirhakah was defeated, and retreated to the south; the Assyrian king annexed the whole country, portioning it out into twenty districts, over which he placed governors to rule, as vassals in his name. Then, concluding a treaty with Tirhakah, he returned to Nineveh. Soon after he fell sick, and associated his son Assur-bani-pal in the government. It is from the records left by the latter that we learn the proceedings both of his father and of himself in Egypt. Tirhakah, probably on hearing of the illness of Esar-haddon, emerged from his retreat, and advancing north, regardless of his treaty, occupied Memphis, and expelled the Assyrian garrisons and governors. They fled to Nineveh, and told what had happened; Assur-bani-pal immediately assembled a large army, and entered Egypt. 'When Tirhakah had heard in the city of Memphis of the approach of my army,' says the king, 'he numbered his hosts, and drew them up in battle array. In a fierce battle he was put to flight. Fear seized upon him, and he escaped from Memphis, the city of his honour, and fled away in ships to save himself alive. He came to Nia, to the great city. I sent my servants after him; a journey of one month and ten days. Then he left Thebes, the city of his empire, and went up the river. My soldiers made a slaughter in that city.' Assur-ban-ipal then reinstated the governors in their respective districts, and returned to Nineveh with great spoil. But Tirhakah, undaunted by defeat, came forth once more from the Nubian hills, and the vassal governors entered into a league with him. Many of them were Egyptian by birth, and unwilling subjects of the Assyrian king, and all were for the moment more afraid of Tirhakah, who was so near at hand, than of the distant power of Assyria. News, however, soon reached Nineveh of what was going on. Letters had been intercepted by 'judges,' and the insurgent vassals were sent to Nineveh bound hand and foot in chains. Assur-bani-pal once more took the field, breathing vengeance and slaughter. He found it politic, however, to restore Necho,[1] prince of Memphis, chief

---

[1] He was an Egyptian, and son of Tafnekht, who headed the league of northern chiefs against Piankhi (p. 246).

of the rebellious vassals, and to uphold him against Tirhakah. But the hand of the Assyrian was heavy on the land. 'Memphis, Sais, Mendes, and Zoan,' he says, 'and all the cities they had led away with them, I took by storm, putting to death both small and great.' Soon after this the gallant Tirhakah died, after a reign of twenty-six years, and his successor, Urdamaneh, following in his steps, occupied Thebes, and once more attempted to wrest Egypt from the invader. Assur-bani-pal took the field in person, and again compelled his foe to retire to the far south. On Thebes he took dire vengeance. 'My warriors attacked the city, and razed it to the ground like a thunderbolt.' Thebes certainly was not 'razed to the ground,' as the proud conqueror boasts, but the destruction was terrible, and the city never recovered the blow. 'Gold and silver, the treasures of the land, precious stones, horses, men and women, huge apes from the mountains—my soldiers took out of the midst of the city as spoil. They brought it to Nineveh, the city of my dominion, and they kissed my feet.' Not far from Nineveh there was living at this time an exile from Israel, who may himself have seen the Egyptian prisoners and the spoil of Thebes. In his indignant denunciation of Nineveh and her king, he thus addresses the magnificent and cruel city: 'Art thou better than No-Amon " (the city of Amen = Thebes)," that was enthroned among the streams, and the floods were round about her; her rampart was upon the river, and the waters her defence. Ethiopia and Egypt were her strength, and it was infinite; Put and Lubim were her helpers. Yet was she carried away and went into captivity; her young children were dashed in pieces at the top of all the streets: they cast lots for her honourable men, and her great men were bound with chains' (Nahum iii. 8-10).[1]

It was little more than half a century later that Nineveh herself fell with a mightier and more overwhelming destruction.

[1] In this and in other quotations from the Old Testament the renderings of Ewald and Stanley have sometimes been adopted.

CHAPTER XIV.

Psammetichus and the Saite Dynasty—The Persian Conquest
—Last Independent Dynasties. (666-340 B.C.)

AFTER the capture and sack of Thebes, the successors of Tirhakah made no further attempts to recover their lost dominion. The princes who ruled in the north, more or less as the vassals of Assyria, were often engaged in mutual strife, and the twenty satrapies established there by Esar-haddon had dwindled down to twelve—the 'Dodecarchy,' of Greek writers. Bravest and most conspicuous amongst the twelve princes was Psamtek (Psammetichus), son of that Necho who had been imprisoned and restored by Assur-bani-pal[1] (p.260). Banished by the jealousy of his rivals, Psammetichus[2] determined on a new and energetic

[1] And thus a descendant of Tafnekht, the ambitious prince of Sais, defeated by Piankhi (p. 246).
[2] The story told by Herodotus is that an oracle had declared that that prince who should make libation out of a brazen goblet should reign over all Egypt. One day all the princes appeared to offer

policy. He formed an alliance with the king of Lydia, and obtained the assistance of a large number of Greek mercenaries—chiefly Carians and Ionians by birth. He resolved, by their aid, to win back the independence of Egypt by driving out the Assyrians, and to reunite the divided land, by bringing it all under his own sceptre. At Momemphis he defeated the Assyrians in a great battle, and they left Egypt to return no more. Assur-bani-pal, who had conquered Egypt and devastated Thebes, was still reigning at Nineveh; and it must have been not a little humiliating to his pride, to be unable to make another attempt to regain what he had lost. But the time had come when Assyria had no soldiers to spare for foreign conquests; they were all wanted at home to defend the monarchy. Weakened by the in-

sacrifice, but the high priest by mistake brought only eleven golden vessels, whereupon Psammetichus took off his helmet and used it for the libation. When it was observed that the oracle had thus, though inadvertently, been fulfilled, it was thought a prudent measure to depose and banish Psammetichus. He consulted the oracle, which announced that vengeance would come by brazen men, showing themselves from seaward. When he heard of pirates clad in brazen armour who had showed themselves in the Delta, he perceived the meaning of the oracle. By enlisting the Greek mercenaries in their panoplies of brass, he accordingly triumphed over his rivals, expelled the Assyrians, and became king of all Egypt.

cessant warfare that had won so triumphant a military ascendency, she was assailed on every side by the nations to whom she had long been a terror, and by her own subject provinces, ever restlessly eager to cast off the yoke of her tyranny.

Meanwhile Psammetichus successfully achieved the other portion of his task; he reunited the north under his sway, and made peace with the rulers of the south. The descendants of the priest-king, of Piankhi and of Tirhakah henceforth made Napata the centre of their dominion, and abandoned all thought of ruling even in Upper Egypt. The friendship thus formed was cemented by the marriage of Psammetichus with a princess of the southern dynasty. She was daughter of a king named Piankhi and his beautiful wife Ameniritis: a statue of her has been preserved, of which Brugsch says, "Sweet peace seems to hover about her features; the very flowers in her hand suggest her high mission as the reconciler of the long feud.'

Under the Saite[1] dynasty, established by

[1] Sais, in the Delta, was a magnificent city, and the temple of the goddess Neith, who was worshipped there, was celebrated for its splendour. The worship of Neith goes back to the earliest times, but

Psammetichus, Egypt enjoyed peace and prosperity for more than a century. The sun of her former greatness had indeed set, but under Psammetichus and his successors she enjoyed a long and brilliant after-glow of light. This period, which has been called the Egyptian *renaissance*, was distinguished by a revival of art, tasteful and refined in character.

Psammetichus never forgot how much he owed to the Greek mercenaries; he gave them land, encouraged them to settle in Egypt, and, in short, showed them so much favour that, Herodotus tells us, the jealousy of the native soldiery was aroused; they deserted the camp in large numbers, and took refuge within the Ethiopian dominions, now become more essentially Egyptian than many parts of Egypt proper. Nor was the king content with showing favour to the mercenaries to whom he owed his crown; he also threw the country open to foreign com-

under the dynasty which had its seat at Sais it attained very great prominence. Neith was a nature-goddess, and was called the 'mother of the sun.' She represents the hidden and mysterious ground of all things, and hence was naturally regarded as the goddess of wisdom. Like Athena, to whom the Greeks compared her, she was at the same time goddess of war. Over her temple was the inscription: 'I am what is, what shall be, and what has been, and no man hath lifted my veil; I am the great mother of Ra.'

merce of every kind. Greek factories were built, and Greek merchants settled in Egypt in large numbers, more especially at Naukratis, which became the emporium of Greek trade. In spite of the favour they showed to foreigners neither Psammetichus nor his successors neglected the national religion and the national superstitions. They cared for the temples, and when an Apis died they buried him with lavish and extraordinary magnificence. The long reign of Psammetichus (666-612) was distinguished by one military enterprise, the taking of Azotus, after a prolonged siege of twenty-nine years. And it was during his reign that the devastating hordes of the Scythians from the far north poured over the Assyrian provinces like a countless swarm of locusts, leaving ruin and desolation behind. They approached the confines of Egypt, but Psammetichus succeeded in buying them off; they may have been sated with plunder and spoil, or may not have cared to undertake the hard and weary journey through the waterless Sinai desert. They disappeared from sight suddenly as they had come into sight, but their terrible onslaught and the havoc they wrought was a fatal blow to Assyria's declining power. It was at the crisis of her fall that Necho (612-596) ascended the throne of Egypt.

Babylon, Elam, and Arabia, leagued against Assyria about 650 B.C., had been successively defeated by King Assur-bani-pal, who took Babylon itself 648 B.C. A pause ensued, for it was no light task to encounter the Assyrian even in the hour of his decline; but on the death of Assur-bani-pal there appears to have been a revolt of some kind, and Nabopolassar, a general who succeeded in putting it down, was made ruler of Babylon by the king of Nineveh. But the ambitious Nabopolassar formed an alliance with the king of Media, and their combined attack was the death-blow of the Assyrian monarchy. It was, perhaps, through a common understanding with the allied states that Psammetichus had besieged Azotus, which lay on the old military road by the sea-coast. Necho took a more active part, and led his army as far as the Euphrates. Whilst on the march, Josiah, king of Judah, had rashly come out to offer him battle, and had been defeated and slain at Megiddo. It must have been at this crisis that

Nineveh fell; but though her fall must have shaken the earth no record has come to us concerning it—its precise date is unknown. Only in the exultant cry of a Hebrew prophet[1] do we hear any echo of the shout of execration and the outburst of triumph that went up as the great city fell :—

'Nineveh is laid waste! who will bemoan her? Whence shall I seek for comforters for thee? ... There is no healing of thy hurt; thy wound is incurable: all that hear of thee shall clap their hands over thee: for upon whom hath not thy wickedness passed continually?'

Upon the ruins of Assyria the genius of Nebuchadnezzar, son of Nabopolassar, raised that mighty Babylonian empire which for about seventy years ruled over the conquered nations. Babylon had never before been distinguished as an ambitious or aggressive state, but the force and energy of this mighty monarch has made her name synonymous with imperial strength, magnificence, and pride. For a brief space Necho had occupied the scene of the triumphs of Thothmes and of Rameses; he

---

[1] Nahum iii. 7, 19; 'No spark of pity mingles with the prophet's delight.'—Stanley, *Jewish Church*.

deposed the successor of Josiah at Jerusalem, and made Jehoiakim king of Judah. But if he had been visited by any flattering visions of a revival of Egyptian empire they were soon rudely dispelled. The young king of Babylon attacked and routed the Egyptian army, which was encamped at Karchemish, on the Euphrates, and forced Necho to retreat within the boundaries of Egypt. The invasion and the repulse of the Egyptian king has been vividly portrayed in the pages of Jewish prophecy. 'Egypt riseth up like the river, his waters are moved like the floods; and he saith, I will go up and will cover the earth; I will destroy the city, with the inhabitants thereof.'[1] The horses and chariots are arrayed for battle, the well-equipped mercenary troops stand in serried ranks; but it was all in vain. 'Wherefore have I seen them dismayed and turned back? their mighty ones have fled apace, and look not back. . . . They said, Arise and let us go again to our own people, and to the land of our nativity, from the oppressing sword.'[2]

It was not only by this ambitious enterprise, and by its utter failure, that Necho's reign was

[1] Jer. xlvi. 8, 9.   [2] Jer. xlvi. 5, 16.

distinguished. He had been compelled to abandon the attempt to construct a canal across the isthmus between the Red Sea and the Mediterranean, but a naval expedition that he sent out was more successful. The vessels were manned by Phœnicians, and, starting from the Red Sea, returned to Egypt in three years' time by way of the Mediterranean, having circumnavigated Africa and noted with amazement that during the first part of their voyage the sun had risen on their left, but afterwards it had risen to the right. To the Greeks of a later day this fact appeared to be on the face of it so incredible that they doubted the truth of the whole story. To us it only affords an additional reason for believing it.

Psammetichus II., the successor of Necho, reigned only about five years, and was followed by Uahpra (or Apries, the *Hophra* of the Old Testament). The aid of this king was sought both from east and west. After the defeat of Necho, and the homeward flight of the Egyptian army, no military expedition had been undertaken. 'The king of Egypt came not again any more out of his land; for the king of

Babylon had taken from the river of Egypt unto the river Euphrates all that pertained to the king of Egypt.'[1] For a moment indeed, Apries seemed to be moved by the cry for aid that came from Jerusalem. In his triumphal march of successful conquest, Nebuchadnezzar had besieged the city, and carried off its king and many others as prisoners to Babylon; he had then placed Zedekiah on the throne, after exacting from him a solemn oath of fealty. But in an evil moment the vassal king rebelled, and, in the hope that is sometimes born of desperation, sent ambassadors into Egypt 'that they might give him horses and much people' (see Ezekiel xvii. 11-21). Irritated by the successive acts of submission and revolt, Nebuchadnezzar now advanced upon the unhappy little country of Judah, which had come to be the sport, as it were, of two mighty states, and resolved to make an end of it altogether. The hope of Zedekiah came to naught; only for a brief interval was the siege suspended, by the news that an Egyptian army was on the march. Soon after, however, it

---

[1] 2 Kings xxiv. 7.

was resumed, and, after it had lasted eighteen months, Jerusalem fell with a sad and terrible destruction—by famine, fire, and slaughter (588 B.C.) The only aid actually rendered by Egypt was the shelter given to the fugitives who sought refuge there after the murder of Gedaliah, the governor appointed by the king of Babylon. They dreaded the vengeance of Nebuchadnezzar; they were weary of suffering, and said one to another: 'We will go into the land of Egypt, where we shall see no war, nor hear the sound of the trumpet, nor have hunger of bread, and there will we dwell.' And in Egypt they took refuge in spite of the remonstrances of the prophet Jeremiah, whom they forced to accompany them.

The Egyptian army, whose advance had momentarily raised the siege of Jerusalem appears to have taken Gaza, but to have retired without encountering the Babylonians. Another expedition was despatched to the west in aid of the Libyans. The Greek colony at Cyrene had received a large number of new settlers, and they had established themselves by dispossessing the natives of their lands.

S

Apries sent an army composed of native Egyptians[1] against Cyrene, but they were defeated, and this defeat was followed by a military revolt. The mutineers complained that they had been selected for the expedition in order that the loss might fall on them, rather than on the Greek mercenaries. The king sent an officer, named Amasis, to the camp, who was popular with the soldiery, and they immediately saluted him as king. Apries then sent a general, named Patahbeni, with orders to bring Amasis back a prisoner, but Amasis replied: 'Tell the king that I will myself lead the army to his very feet.' Apries was so enraged at the ill success of his messenger, that he ordered the unfortunate man's nose and ears to be cut off (a punishment intended for the lowest traitors). This brutal act only incensed the soldiery still further, and the whole army joined in the revolt. Apries, with his Greek mercenaries, met them at Momemphis, but was defeated, and fell into the hands of Amasis, who at first treated him with kindness and

---

[1] It was natural not to send Greeks against their fellow-countrymen, though the action was otherwise interpreted.

respect, but the people murmured at this leniency, and Amasis yielded. Apries was strangled, but his body was buried with due ceremonial in his own sepulchre. Such is the narrative of Greek writers, but there seem some grounds for assuming that the real story was somewhat different; that the king of Babylon himself was at that time in Egypt, and that it was his hand that deposed and slew king Apries and placed Amasis on the throne (572 B.C.). The new king showed even greater favour to the Greeks than his predecessors had done. He gave them possession of the town of Naukratis, with all rights of local self-government and religious worship. Four Greek temples were erected there by different Grecian nationalities. Amasis also sent gifts to Delphi and other Grecian shrines, and he married Ladice of Cyrene, a Greek by birth. He formed alliances with Crœsus of Lydia, and Polycrates of Samos, and his own body-guard was composed of Greek mercenaries.

Whether or not Amasis had ascended the throne as a vassal of Babylon, he certainly reigned as an independent monarch. Nebuchadnezzar, after spending more than thirty years in warfare and in conquest, passed the concluding years of his reign in splendid luxury in the city which he had raised to be the head of the nations, and the glory and wonder of the world. 'Is not this great Babylon which I have built? I have made completely strong the defences of Babylon; may it last for ever!' It was only three years after his death that Cyrus resolved to free Persia from the dominion of Media; he accomplished this task after a hard struggle, and then embarked upon that career of conquest which only paused after the eventful night when Babylon, given up to careless revelry, was taken by a foe who could 'show no mercy' (539 B.C.). Surprise was mingled with exultation as, at the cry, 'Babylon is taken,' 'the earth trembled, and the sound was heard amongst the nations.' 'How is the praise of the whole earth surprised! How is Babylon become an astonishment—a desolation among the nations!'

But the nations were not free although the empire of Nebuchadnezzar had fallen; they had but exchanged masters. The ambition of the conqueror was not sated; the enthusiasm excited by his genius and his triumphs amongst his hardy, warlike, and uncultured followers, did not ebb when Babylon had fallen. There is little doubt that Cyrus planned the invasion of Egypt which was carried out by his son Cambyses[1] (527 B.C.).

Amasis, who had been raised to the throne by so unexpected a stroke of fortune, was a genial and pleasure-loving man—fond of the wine-cup and the merry jest, but he governed Egypt well and prudently during a reign of more than forty years. When he died he bequeathed to his son Psammetichus III. 'the inheritance of a lost kingdom.'[2] The Persians entered Egypt, and in a desperate battle at

---

[1] The story of Herodotus is that an Egyptian oculist had been sent to Persia to cure the king, who was suffering from some complaint of the eyes. Cambyses heard so much from him of the beauty of the daughter of Amasis, that he desired to have her for his wife. Amasis, unwilling to send his own daughter, substituted the daughter of his predecessor Apries. Cambyses, on discovering the fraud, was so enraged that he undertook the invasion of Egypt to punish the perfidy of its king. Cambyses certainly was not the man to wait for a pretext, whether the story be true or not. The narratives of Herodotus are by no means to be relied on; all that he relates as an eye-witness is of the utmost value.

[2] Brugsch, *History of Egypt*.

Pelusium the Egyptians were defeated; Memphis was then captured with great slaughter. The unfortunate Psammetichus, who had only reigned six months, was taken prisoner; it is said that he was put to death later on upon a charge of conspiracy. Cambyses assumed an Egyptian title, and reigned over the land as the first monarch of the twenty-seventh, or Persian dynasty. He appears at first to have treated his new subjects with forbearance; he visited the celebrated temple at Sais, inquired into the rites and mysteries of the worship of Neith, and redressed certain grievances of which the priests complained.[1] But to the passionate ambition of Cambyses, the possession of Egypt was only a stepping-stone to the accomplishment of other and far-reaching schemes. He designed to march westward against the rising city of Carthage; to occupy the oasis of Amen, and to conquer the kingdom of Ethiopia. But his Phœnician mercenaries refused to be led against their kinsmen at Carthage; the army,

[1] It was Uah-hor-penres, priest of Neith, of whom Cambyses inquired, and who seems to have won great respect from the king. Sais appears, through his influence and good offices, to have been 'saved in the great calamity that fell upon the land.'

50,000 strong, which he despatched across the desert, was lost in the burning sands, and the forces which he himself led against Ethiopia were repulsed, and suffered terribly on the retreat from the ravages of famine. The survivors appear to have vented some of their ill-will upon the monuments and statues of Thebes as they passed through on the way to Memphis. The mood in which Cambyses entered that city may be imagined; mortified and exasperated as he was, he found the whole city given up to festivities and rejoicings, and concluded that they must be celebrating his disastrous defeat. Thereupon his fury turned to madness; and when he heard that the people were celebrating the finding of an Apis, he ordered the priests to be scourged, and the chief men of the city to be slain. Then he ordered the sacred bull to be brought into his presence, and stabbed him with his own dagger. There can be little doubt that in an access of madness, Cambyses wrought terrible havoc on the temples and monuments of the land, though he may not have been guilty of all that was laid to his charge by a people who execrated his memory, and regarded his madness as the just visitation of Heaven. But suddenly there came news of an insurrection in Persia, and Cambyses instantly started for his capital. At Ecbatana, as he was mounting his horse, he stabbed himself (voluntarily or accidentally) with his own dagger—with the same weapon with which he had killed the Apis, the awe-struck Egyptians told Herodotus, and in the very same part of the body.

The short but terrible tyranny of Cambyses was over, and Darius, who succeeded in 522 B.C., proved a mild and forbearing ruler. But after his defeat by the Athenians at Marathon, the Egyptians rose in revolt; Xerxes had to put down this insurrection before he too went against Greece.

During the two centuries when hostilities were so often renewed between Persians and Greeks, there was friendship between Egypt and Greece, and not unfrequently alliance against the Persian kings. The relations between these two countries had long been of a friendly character. Egypt representing all that was wisest and greatest in the long æon that was closing, Greece representing all that was brightest and fairest in the era that was opening. Homer already knew, concerning Egypt, that it was a fertile and a wealthy land—a land especially famed for the skill of its physicians; he tells of its 'god-descended stream,' and of the Isle of Pharos, with the safe anchorage by it afforded to storm-tossed mariners. Nor was he ignorant of Thebes in the far south, and her imperial magnificence—Egyptian Thebes, the 'treasure-house of countless wealth, who boasts her hundred gates—through each of which with horse and car two hundred warriors march.'[1]

To the Egyptians of Homer's time, the Greeks were probably known as roving pirates of the Mediterranean; afterwards, by a natural transition, as mercenary troops—later on, as busy and successful merchants. Greeks, however, visited Egypt on nobler errands than the mere pursuit of wealth. In the reign of Amasis, Solon, the Athenian lawgiver, resided for a while both at the 'city of the Sun,' the most ancient seat of Egyptian learning, and at Sais, the

[1] Lord Derby's translation.

sanctuary of the goddess of wisdom. To him it was that an old Egyptian priest, who was his friend, addressed the memorable words—'O Solon! Solon! you Greeks are ever children; having no ancient opinion nor any discipline of long standing.' The earliest Greek philosophers, Pythagoras of Samos, and Thales of Miletus, were believed to have visited Egypt, and no doubt their eager restless inquiries also seemed to the Egyptians like those of 'children,' who can so easily ask more than the wisest man can ever answer.

Nothing could be more natural, or indeed inevitable, than that the awakening intellectual and artistic life of Greece should be strongly attracted towards the ancient wisdom and civilisation of Egypt.[1] Geometric and other scientific ideas they certainly carried home from the Land of the Pyramids, and the rudiments of their own civilisation and learning were always said by the Greeks to have come from Egypt.

Persia had conquered Egypt, and was

[1] 'All intellectual Greeks,' says Grote, 'were naturally attracted to go and visit the wonders on the banks of the Nile.'

threatening Greece, but the invasion of Xerxes was triumphantly repulsed, and the Athenians subsequently sent aid to the Egyptians in their renewed attempt to cast off the yoke of the common foe.

The revolt was at first successful, but on the arrival of Persian reinforcements the Athenians were driven from Memphis, and forced to retire to an island on the Nile. Here they were blockaded for eighteen months; the foe then, diverting the river from its course, took the Athenian camp by storm, and a fleet of fifty Athenian ships, which entered the Nile in ignorance of the disastrous turn of events, fell into the hands of the Persians. Amyrtæus, who had been proclaimed king, took flight, and sought refuge in the inaccessible marshes of the Delta.

Thus Egypt passed once more under the Persian yoke, but the Persian power itself was declining, and Amyrtæus of Sais (the grandson of the Amyrtæus who fled to the marshes) made himself King of Egypt. His reign of six years constitutes the twenty-eighth dynasty.

This was succeeded by the twenty-ninth (of Mendes), and the thirtieth (of Sebennytus). Under these, her last native dynasties, Egypt maintained her recovered independence for sixty years, during which period she sent aid both to the Lacedæmonians and to the king of Cyprus, in the long protracted conflict with Persia. Art also revived once more, and was distinguished by a grace and finish that seem to speak of Grecian influences.

Under one of the kings of the thirtieth dynasty, Agesilaus of Sparta was invited to command the Egyptian army. It is said that on his arrival the Egyptians were taken by surprise to find so renowned a king and warrior 'a little deformed old man, clad in mean attire, and regardless of show and luxury,' who 'would sit carelessly upon the grass amongst his soldiers.'[1] At any rate they only intrusted him with the command of the mercenaries. Angry at the affront, the Spartan king supported a rival prince, who displaced Takos, the reigning sovereign, and assumed his place. This king, Nectanebus (361 B.C.), was the last of

[1] Grote.

the long line of kings that opens with king Mena.

Ochus, a cruel but energetic sovereign, succeeded Artaxerxes II. on the Persian throne; the energies of Greece were concentrated in the struggle against Philip of Macedon. Ochus invaded Egypt with an immense army (ten thousand of whom were Greek mercenaries!). Nectanebus was an incompetent general, but, confident of his own ability, he commanded in person the army of Egyptians and Greek mercenaries, who encountered the Persians at Pelusium. He was defeated, and instantly fled to Memphis; on hearing of the further progress of the enemy, he quitted Memphis and fled southward, until he reached the safe shelter of the Ethiopian land. With this hurried and ignominious retreat, the ancient monarchy of Egypt ceased to be. Deprived of their king and leader, the people at once submitted (about 340 B.C.).

But the Persian conquerors only ruled for twelve years longer—years of danger and distress for their country. Greece had been subjugated by Macedon, and Alexander, son of

Philip, rapidly conquered the Persian provinces. Egypt alone remained; in 332 B.C., he entered that country, where he met with no resistance, but was rather hailed as a deliverer. He went to Memphis, where he offered sacrifice to the Apis. Alexander also visited the temple of Amen (of Zeus Ammon, the Greeks called it), in the oasis, twelve days' journey from Memphis, and in the heart of the desert. This temple was of great renown in antiquity, and its oracle was consulted far and wide. The conqueror was received by the priests with the most flattering assurances. He was the 'son of Zeus,' they told him, and should 'pursue his career of victory until he was taken to the gods.'

Before quitting Egypt, Alexander planned the foundation of the city that was destined to be so famed in after times both as an emporium of trade and as a school of learning and philosophy—Alexandria.

The battle of Arbela decided the fate of the Persian monarchy. But Alexander did not live to rule long over the empire he had won; on his death his dominions were divided amongst his successors. Egypt fell to the Ptolemies, and remained under their rule for three hundred years, until 30 B.C., when it became a Roman province.

Sphinx.

APPENDIX I.

TABLE OF DYNASTIES.

DYNASTY I.—THINITE.

Mena.	Hesepti.
Teta.	Merbap.
Atet.	Sememptah.
Ata.	Kebeh.

DYNASTY II.—THINITE.

Betau.	Uatnes.
Kakau.	Senta.
Baienneter.	

DYNASTY III.—MEMPHITE.

Tati.	Teta I.
Bebi.	Setes.
Nebka.	Neferkara.
Sersa.	Senefru.

DYNASTY IV.—MEMPHITE.

Khufu.	Menkaura.
Tetefra.	Aseskaf.
Khafra.	

DYNASTY V.—MEMPHITE.

Userkaf.	Userenra.
Sehura.	Menkauhor.
Kaka.	Tetkara.
Neferarkara.	Unas.

DYNASTY VI.—ELEPHANTINE.

Teta II.	Merienra II.
Userkara.	Neterkara.
Pepi Merira.	Menkara.
Merienra I.	Netakerti
Neferkara I.	(Nitocris).

DYNASTY VII.—MEMPHITE.

No records or names preserved.

DYNASTY VIII.—MEMPHITE.

Neferkara II.	Neferkahor.
Neferkara Nebi.	Neferkara V.
Tetkara.	Seneferka Annu.
Neferkara III.	. . . Kaura.
Merenhor.	Neferkaura.
Seneferka.	Neferkauhor.
Enkara.	Neferarkara.
Neferkara IV.	

DYNASTIES IX. AND X.
(HERACLEOPOLIS.)

Probably contemporary with foregoing. Names unknown.

DYNASTY XI.—THEBAN.

Ten kings—amorgst them the **Antefs** and Mentuhoteps. Egypt re-united **under** last two kings of this dynasty:

Nebtaura.   Sankhkara.

DYNASTY XII.—THEBAN.

Amenemhat I.	Amenemhat III.
Usertesen I.	Amenemhat IV.
Amenemhat II.	Sebeknefrura
Usertesen II.	(Queen).
Usertesen III.	

DYNASTY XIII.—THEBAN.

Sebekhotep I.
Six successors bearing same name.

APPENDIX.

DYNASTY XIV.—XOITE.
Seventy-six kings ruling in 184 years.

DYNASTIES XV. AND XVI.
The Hyksos Kings.

DYNASTY XVII.—THEBAN.
Native rulers in the south—at first tributary to Hyksos Kings.
War of liberation by—
Sekenenra. Taa-aa. Taa-ken.

DYNASTY XVIII.—THEBAN.

Aahmes.	Amenhotep III.
Amenhotep I.	Amenhotep IV.
Thothmes I.	Khu-en-aten.
Thothmes II.	Saanekht.
Hatasu.	Tutankhamen.
Thothmes III.	Ai.
Amenhotep II.	Horus.
Thothmes IV.	

DYNASTY XIX.—THEBAN.

Rameses I.	Seti Menephtah II.
Seti I.	Amenmeses.
Rameses II.	Siptah.
Menephtah I.	Setnekht.

DYNASTY XX.—THEBAN.
Rameses III.
Ten or more successors of the same name.

DYNASTY XXI.—PRIEST-KINGS.

Herhor.	Pinotem II.
Piankhi.	Menkheperra.
Pinotem I.	Pinotem III.

DYNASTY XXII.—BUBASTITE.

Sheshenk I. (Shishak.)	Sheshenk II.
	Takeleth II.
Usarken I.	Sheskenk III.
Takeleth I.	Pimai.
Usarken II.	Sheshenk IV.

DYNASTY XXIII.—TANITE.
Petubast. Usarken III. Psemaut.

DYNASTY XXIV.—SAITE.
Bakenrenef.
Petty rulers in Delta.

DYNASTY XXV.—ETHIOPIAN.

Shebek (Sabaco).	Taharak (Tirhakah).
Piankhi.	Rutamen.
Nutmeramen.	

DYNASTY XXVI.—SAITE.
Psemtek I. (P'sammetichus).
Nekau (Necho).
Psemtek II.
Uahabra (Apries).
Aahmes II. (Amasis).
Psemtek III.

DYNASTY XXVII.—PERSIAN.
Cambyses and six successors.

DYNASTY XXVIII.—SAITE.
Amyrtæus.

DYNASTY XXIX.—MENDESIAN.

Naifaaret I.	Psemant.
Haker.	Naifaaret II.

DYNASTY XXX.—SEBENNYTE.
Nekhthorheb (Nectanebo).
Tether.
Nekhtnebef.

This list, with some slight variations, follows that given by Sir Erasmus Wilson as an appendix to 'EGYPT OF THE PAST.'

APPENDIX II.

DECIPHERMENT OF THE HIEROGLYPHS.

The idea long prevailed that the hieroglyphic characters were ideographic—*i.e.* that they represented ideas, not sounds; and any attempt at decipherment was hopeless. Before the end of last century, however, a hint had been thrown out that the characters might prove to be phonetic—*i.e.* representing sounds like the letters of our ordinary alphabets. And a further suggestion had been offered that the words enclosed within ovals might be the names of royal personages. But unless some means existed of comparing those names with the same names written in a known language, not a single hieroglyph could be read. The discovery of the Rosetta stone in 1799 supplied the means required. On that stone was engraved an inscription in three characters—the hieroglyphic, the demotic or popular Egyptian, and the Greek. Scholars, however, turned their attention at first rather to the comparison of the demotic and the Greek, as the idea still prevailed that the hieroglyphs were not phonetic. It happened, also, that the beginning of the hieroglyphic and the end of the Greek inscription were wanting, which added greatly to the difficulty of comparing the texts. Thus 'the seals of the mysterious book were still unclosed' when Champollion began his labours. He succeeded in identifying the names of Ptolemy and Cleopatra, and by comparing them with each other and with their Greek counterparts he identified ten letters which were clearly phonetic. The first and second characters in the king's name were found in their right places in that of the queen, and the initial letter of Cleopatra did not occur in the name of Ptolemy, etc. By the examination and comparison of other proper names other letters were determined, and a phonetic alphabet gradually acquired. But the formidable task remained of examining, reducing to order, and deciphering the vast mass of characters that were still unread.

The fact is that in the Egyptian hieroglyphic writing, hundreds of characters are employed as well as the letters of the alphabet; these characters represent syllables, words, or ideas, and could be used instead of the letters, almost at the pleasure of the writer. This gradually became apparent to Champollion, and as, fortunately, there are a very great number of copies extant of the same MSS., he was able, by laborious and persevering collation of those MSS., to determine the phonetic value of a great number of characters. To use a familiar illustration, it is as though two copies of an English sentence were compared by a foreigner who was acquainted only with the alphabet; in one of them occurred the word *three* and the word *and*, whilst in the other copy, in the places occupied by those words, appeared the character 3 and the character &; or in an astronomical treatise, he would find the words *sun* and *Taurus* interchangeable with the signs ☉ and ♉. It would clearly be possible for him to read the four signs into the words for which they respectively stand, by a comparison of copies. The only difference is that the use of signs, whether for syllables, words, or ideas, is carried to such an immense extent in the old Egyptian writing, that their decipherment was a work of the most arduous kind. Champollion, nevertheless, succeeded in recovering and reading the old Egyptian language to a great extent, and his work has been ardently carried forward by his successors. The language, however, even when deciphered and read, must have remained unintelligible, if modern Coptic (the descendant of the ancient tongue) had not afforded the key to its translation.

INDEX.

AAHMES, conqueror of the Hyksos, 87, 93.
—— his mummy discovered, 94.
Aahmes, admiral of the fleet, exploits of, 90 *seq.*
Aah-hotep, queen, 87.
Aarsu, the Syrian, 210.
Abydos, shrine of Osiris, 6.
—— ruins of, 10, 11.
—— tablet of, 151.
—— visit of Rameses II. to, 152 *seq.*
Abu-simbel, rock temples and colossal statues at, 166, 167.
Agesilaus of Sparta in Egypt, 284.
Alexander the Great in Egypt, 286.
Alexandria founded, 286.
Amasis, King; his policy and character, 275, 277.
Amen, god of Thebes, 49, 132, 223.
Amen-Ra, hymn to, 222, 223.
Amen, great temple of, at Thebes, (Karnak), 55, 65, 95, 128, 151.
Amenemhat I., instructions of, 51 *seq.*
—— conspiracy against, 52, 53.
—— pyramid of, 64.
Amenemhat III. notes rise of Nile, 70.
—— constructs Lake Mœris and the Labyrinth, 71, *seq.*
Amenemhib, inscription of, 112, 123.
Amenhotep I., 93, 94.
Amenhotep II., 124.
Amenhotep III., his campaigns in the South, 128.
—— his buildings at Thebes, 128.

Amenhotep III., colossi of, 129 *seq.*
Amenhotep, architect, 128 *seq.*
Ameni, inscription of, 66, 67.
Amenritis, queen of Ethiopia, 265.
Amenti, scenes in, depicted, 192 *seq.*
Amu, the, 26, 76.
Amyrtæus, 283.
Animal worship, 198 *seq.*
Antef, the family, 43.
—— festal dirge of house of, 44, 45.
Apepi, serpent of evil, 195, 196.
Apepi, Hyksos king; his embassy to the ruler of the South, 83.
Apis, sacred bull of Memphis, 199.
Apis-worship, development of, 243, 244.
Apollonius of Tyana on animal worship, 200 *note.*
Apries, King (Hophra), 272 *seq.*
Ark, the sacred, 179.
Art, excellence and defects of, 201, 202.
Assyrian empire, first, 239.
—— second, rise of, 253.
—— fall of, 269.
Assyrians first enter Egypt, 259.
—— finally expelled, 264.
Assur-bani-pal, king of Assyria, 259 *seq.*
Ata, King, 16.
Aten the Disk, worship of, 133 *seq.*
Atet, Princess, tomb of, 33.
Avaris, fortified by the Hyksos, 81.

INDEX.

Avaris, siege and capture of, 90, 91.
Azotus, siege of, 267.

BABA-ABANA, inscription of, 89.
Babylon, conflicts with Assyria, 215, 239.
—— empire of, 269.
—— fall of, 276.
Bai-en-neter, decree of King, 15.
Bast or Pasht, the goddess, 238 *note*.
Beni-Hassan, rock tombs of, 75.
Biban-el-Moluk ; tombs of the kings, 171.
Book of the 'Manifestation' or 'Coming forth into Day'; commonly called 'Book' or 'Ritual of the Dead,' 10.
Bubastis, city of, 238.

CAMBYSES invades and conquers Egypt, 277.
—— his disaster, cruelty and madness, 279.
—— his end, 280.
Chaldea, early civilisation of, 215.
Columns, Hall of, at Karnak, 151.
Confession, the Negative, 67, 68.
Crown, double, of Egypt, 16.
Cyrene, Greek colony of, 273.
Cyrus, King, 276.

DARIUS, king of Persia, 280.
Dodecarchy, the, 263.

ESAR-HADDON, king of Assyria, 259.

FAMINE, many years of, 89.
Fayoum, oasis of, 70.
Funeral celebrations, 39, 190, 191.

GHIZEH, pyramids of, 18 *seq.*
Gods, representation of, 119, 192 *seq.*
Greece, early, as known to the Egyptians, 281.
—— influence of Egypt on, 282.
—— alliances between Egypt and, 280, 283, 284.

Greek mercenaries, 264, 266.
Greek merchants and colonists, 267, 273.

HAMMAMAT, valley of, 46, 149.
Hanno, expedition of, 47.
Harper, Lay of the, 191, 192.
Hatasu, Queen ; her pride and ambition, 96.
—— splendid temple of, 97.
—— her expedition to Punt, 99 *seq.*
Hebrew colonists in Goshen, 89.
—— reduced to bondage, 204.
—— exodus of, 205.
Herodotus, the historian, 44, 69, 71, 200, 218, 263, 266, 277.
Her-hor, priest-king, his family vault, 230, 234.
Herusha, the, 26, 27.
Hezekiah, alliance with Tirhakah, 256, 257.
Homer, his acquaintance with Egypt, 281.
Hophra, *see* Apries.
Horse, first appearance of, 80.
Horus, the god, son of Isis, 3 *seq.*
Horus, King, 139.
Houses and gardens, 180 *seq.*
Hyksos, invasion of, 80.
—— rule and expulsion of, 81 *seq.*

IMMIGRANTS, Asiatic, 76, 77.
Invocation, customary funeral, 39.
Isis, the goddess, 2 *seq.*
—— *Lamentations of*, 2 *seq.*
Israelites in Canaan, 215.
Israelitish empire, 241.

JEREMIAH in Egypt, 273.
Jerusalem, siege and destruction f, 273.
Jeroboam in Egypt, 242.
Joseph in Egypt, 89.
Josiah, King, 268.

INDEX.

KADESH, battle of, 159.
Kames, Prince, 86.
Karchemish, battle of, 270.
Khafra, pyramid and statue of, 23.
Khamus, Prince, priest of Apis, 199.
Khem, 'lord of the mountain,' 49.
Khemi, a name of Egypt, 69.
Kheta (Hittites), campaign of Seti I. against, 144.
—— war of Rameses II. with, 156 seq.
—— treaty of Rameses with, 169 seq.
Khetasir, king of Kheta, 156, 168, 169.
Khnumhotep, family and tomb of, 75.
Khons, the god, 49, 222 note.
—— oracle-temple of, 222, 225.
—— visit of, to Bakhten, 227, seq.
Khufu, great pyramid of, 22, 23.
Khu-en-aten, new religion of, 133.
—— family life of, 135, 136.
Kom-es-Sultan, mound of, 11.
Koptos, town of, 46, 214.

LABYRINTH, THE, 71.
Lebanon, visit of Seti I. to, 145.
Libyan invasion of Egypt, 207 seq.
Luxor, temple of, 128, 175.

MAGIC, practice of, 221, 222.
Manetho, the historian, 81 note.
Marmaiu, Libyan king, 207.
Mashuasha, defeat of, 213.
Medinet Habou, temple of, 218.
Megiddo, battle of, 109.
Meidoom, early tombs at, 30.
Memnon, statues of, 130.
Memphis, founded by Mena, 12.
Mena, first king of Egypt, 1, 12.
Mendes, ram of, 199.
Menephtah I. defeats the Libyans, 209 seq.

Menkaura, his pyramid and sarcophagus, 24.
Mentuhoteps, princely family of, 46.
Mentuhotep, a great noble, 74, 75.
Mercenary troops, 209, 246, 264.
Merienra, King; sepulchre and mummy of, 25.
Mesopotamia, campaigns in, 94, 110.
Migdol, battle of, 217.
Mines of copper and *mafek*, 17, 65, 214.
Mnevis, sacred bull of Heliopolis, 199.
Mœris, Lake, 71.
Momemphis, battle of, 264.
Morality, standard of, 67, 68.
Moses, 205.
Mut, the Divine Mother, 49.

NAHARINA, see Mesopotamia.
Nahum, the prophet, 262, 269.
Napata, city of, 238, 265.
Necho, Assyrian viceroy at Memphis, 260.
Necho, King, defeated at Karchemish, 270.
—— his naval expedition, 271.
Necropolis of Memphis, 15.
Nectanebus, last native king, 284, 285.
Nefert, Princess, statue of, 34.
Nefermat, tomb of, 33.
Nefertai, wife of Khu-en-aten, 136.
Nefertari, wife of Rameses II., 167.
Neith, the goddess, 265, 266 note.
Negroes (or Nahsi), 12, 69, 128, 165.
Negro queen, visit of, 137.
Nile, Egypt the gift of, 69.
—— rise of, recorded, 70.
—— Hymn to the, 223, 224.
Nineveh, fall of, 269.
Nitocris, Queen, 41.
Nomes, Egypt divided into, 42.
Nubia, added to Egypt, 68.

INDEX

Nut—the Heaven—mother of Osiris, 3 *note*, 25 *note*, 196.
Nut-meramen, King; dream of, 252.

OASIS of Amen, 278, 286.
—— Fayoum, 70.
Obelisks of Heliopolis, 10, 64, 65.
—— of Hatasu, 97.
—— of Thothmes III., 116.
Ochus, King of Persia, 285.
Oracle-temple of Khons, 222, 225.
On (Heliopolis), ancient city of, 7 *seq.*, 64, 250.
Osiris, myth of, and Isis, 2 *seq.*
—— judgment of the spirit before, 5, 67, 192.

PALESTINE or Canaan, land of, 107, 113, 124, 144, 215.
Pa-Ra, City of the Sun, 6, 64, 250.
Pa-Ramessu, city of Rameses, poetical description of, 163, 164.
Pasht or Basht, the goddess, 238 *note*.
Pelusium, battle of, 277.
Pentaur, heroic poem of, 160 *seq.*
Pepi, King; sepulchre and mummy of, 25.
Persian empire, rise of, 276.
Persians first enter Egypt, 277.
—— final conquest by, 285.
Philistines, nation of, 240, 241.
Phœnicians, the, 113, 143, 156, 170, 240.
Phœnix, story of the, 9.
Philo of Alexandria on the sacred animals, 200.
Piankhi, the Ethiopian king, 246.
—— inscription of, 247 *seq.*
Pinotem II., his wife and child, 234.
Pithom, store-city, 205.
—— site of, identified, 205 *note*.
Priesthood of Egypt, 8.
—— growth of power at Thebes, 229.
Priest-kings, 230 *seq.*

Priest-kings, their family tomb, 233.
—— discovery of mummies there, 234 *seq.*
Princess, the possessed, of Bakhten, 226 *seq.*
Prosopis, battle of, 209.
Psamtek (Psammetichus) I., 263.
—— II., 271.
—— III., 277.
Ptah, the god, 2, 12, 208.
Ptah-hotep, maxims of, 34, 35.
Punt; expedition of Sankhkara, 47.
—— of Hatasu, 99, *seq.*
Pyramid builders, 17 *seq.*
Pyramid of Sakkara, 16.
—— the Great, 22, 23.
—— of Khafra, 23.
—— of Menkaura, 24.
—— of Amenemhat I., 64.
Pyramids, construction of, 22, 29, 30.
—— names of, 39.

RA, worship of, at On, 2, 49.
—— his triumph over Apepi, 196.
Raamses, store-city, 205.
Ra-hotep, statue of Prince, 34.
Rameses I., 142.
Rameses II., childhood of, 146.
—— visit to Abydos, 152 *seq.*
—— invocation of his father, 155.
—— war with the Kheta, 156 *seq.*
—— danger and prowess of, 159.
—— campaigns and exploits, 165 *seq.*
—— architectural achievements, 163, 167, 175.
—— colossal statues of, 14, 167.
—— fate of his mummy, 172.
Rameses III., drives back invading tribes, 213.
—— repels great invasion of confederates, 217.
—— victories and spoils, 218.
—— conspiracy against, 220 *seq.*
—— tomb of, 224.

Ramessidæ, successors of Rameses III., 225 *seq.*
Rameses IX., violation of tombs discovered under, 226.
Rameses XII., the god Khons sent to Bakhten by, 226 *seq.*
Ramesseum, the, 189.
Rampsinitus, Rameses III. so called by the Greeks, 218.
Rome, Egypt a province of, 287.

SAIS, city of, 265.
—— visit of Cambyses to, 278.
Sakkara, pyramids of, 16.
Samaria taken by Sargon, 255.
Saneha, story of, 55 *seq.*
San-Tanis or Zoan, 162 *seq.*
Scythians, the, in Asia, 267.
Seb, Earth-god, father of Osiris, 2, 3 *note.*
Sechet, the goddess, *see* Pasht.
Sefek, 'Lady of Writings,' 119.
Sekenen-Ra, a patriot, 85.
Semem-kheftu-ef, tame lion of Rameses, 157, 166, 167.
Semnut, architect of Hatasu, 98.
Senefru, King, 17.
Serapeum, the, 243.
Sesostris, of the Greeks, 220.
Set, brother and foe of Osiris, story of, 2, 3.
Seti I., his campaign in Palestine, 144.
—— against the Kheta, 144 *seq.*
—— triumph of, 145, 147.
—— his Hall of Columns and his temple at Abydos, 151.
Seti Menephtah II., 209.
Setnekht, founder of Dynasty XX., 210, 211.
Shebek, King, (So or Sabaco), 255.
Sheshenk I., (Shishak), 242.
—— his campaign in Judæa, 242, 243.

Slavery in Egypt, 116, 117, 203, 204.
Solomon, king of Israel, 241.
Solon in Egypt, 281, 282.
Sphinx, the Great, 21.
Superstition, growth of, 222.
Symbolism in religion, 197.
Symbols, animals as, 198, 199.

TAA, the family of, 86 *seq.*
Tafnekht, a prince of the north, 24 *seq.*
Tai-ti, Queen, 132, 172.
Ta-khent or Nubia, 68.
Ta-neter, the 'divine land,' 47.
Tel-el-Amarna, site of city of Khu-en-aten, 134.
Temples, Egyptian, 176 *seq.*
Thebes, first mention of, 43.
—— in her magnificence, 186, 187.
—— Western, the City of the Dead, 187 *seq.*
—— sack of, by Assur-bani-pal, 261, 262.
Thi, tomb of, 36, 38.
Thinis-Abydos, twin cities of, 6.
Thoth, the god, 75 *note*, 192.
Thothmes I., campaign in Mesopotamia, 94.
Thothmes II., 96.
Thothmes III., his boyhood, 97.
—— coronation of, 103.
—— enters Palestine, 107.
—— his victorious campaigns in Asia; extent of empire, 109-111.
—— his wealth, and gifts to the temples, 113-115.
—— heroic song in honour of, 120, 121.
—— fate of his mummy, 123, 124.
Thothmes IV., dream of, 125 *seq.*
Tiglath-Pileser, king of Assyria, 253.
Tirhakah, king of Ethiopia and Egypt; his long conflict with Assyria, 259 *seq.*

INDEX.

Trade, manufactures, and amusements of the people, 182-186.
Tum, the god, worship of, 49 *and note.*
Tutankh-amen, King, 137.

Uahpra, *see* Apries.
Uah-hor-penres, priest of Neith, 278 *note.*
Una, inscription of, 26.
Unas, King, 25.
University, ancient, of On, 8.

Usertesen I. associated with his father, 51.
—— his obelisk and other buildings, 64, 65.
Usertesen III., conquers Nubia, 68, 69.

Wady Maghara, mines in the valley of, 17, 65.

Zedekiah, king of Judah, 272.
Zoan, city of, 162 *seq.*, 169, 237, 257.

www.ingramcontent.com/pod-product-compliance
Lightning Source LLC
Chambersburg PA
CBHW030010240426
43672CB00007B/895